From the Horrors of World War II...

to a
Great Love Story

EDITH V. LANDIS

Order this book online at www.trafford.com
or email orders@trafford.com

Most Trafford titles are also available at major online book retailers.

© Copyright 2003 Edith V. Landis.

All rights reserved. No part of this publication may be reproduced, stored in a retrieval system, or transmitted, in any form or by any means, electronic, mechanical, photocopying, recording, or otherwise, without the written prior permission of the author.

Printed in the United States of America.

Landis, Edith V., 1925-
From the horrors of World War II to a great love story / Edith V. Landis.

I. Title.

D811.5.L328 2003   940.53'161'092   C2003-900332-9

ISBN: 978-1-5539-5652-5 (sc)
ISBN: 978-1-4122-5279-9 (e)

Trafford rev. 01/18/2013

   www.trafford.com

North America & international
toll-free: 1 888 232 4444 (USA & Canada)
phone: 250 383 6864 ♦ fax: 812 355 4082

Dedication

This book is dedicated with great love to my daughters, Janet and Debbie, and my son, Steve. You have given me a lot of encouragement to write this story of my life. I am very proud of you, and thank you for all the love, support and caring you have shown me daily. You have made my life worth living.

I also want to dedicate this book in memory of my loving husband, Ardell L. Landis, who passed away in 1998 after fifty-one years of a great marriage. He will live in my heart forever!

A special thanks to my grandsons Bruce, Mick, Justin and Brock, for all the love you have shown me. I am very proud of all of you, and love you very much.

My appreciation to my daughter Janet, Lesa Nornhold and Adam Nornhold, for typing, editing, and all of their efforts; and to Adrienne Beaver for designing this book.

Table of Contents

Foreword 7

Introduction 9

Chapter 1: My Childhood 11

Chapter 2: The Hitler Regime 17

Chapter 3: World War II – The Beginning 25

Chapter 4: Blackouts and Air Raids 34

Chapter 5: The Job 42

Chapter 6: Assassination Attempt 46

Chapter 7: The Battle of Berlin 53

Chapter 8: The Russian Occupation 60

Chapter 9: German Soldiers Return Home 73

Chapter 10: The American Occupation 75

Chapter 11: A Match Made in Heaven 79

Chapter 12: Leaving Berlin 98

Chapter 13: Arrival in America 105

Chapter 14: The Big Adjustment 122

Chapter 15: The Final Chapter 130

Foreword

I was one of the first seven German war brides to receive permission to come to the United States to marry an ex-GI after World War II. I was the first German war bride to come to Pennsylvania. It was such a happy moment when I was finally reunited with my fiancé, Ardell L. Landis, who I would marry a short time later.

Because there was so much attention given to World War II in the last few years, I was asked to speak at several historical societies, and also had speaking engagements at various schools and churches. Everyone who heard my story encouraged me to write a book. This work is the product of that encouragement.

Introduction

This is the true story of my life in Berlin, Germany, during the Hitler Regime, World War II, six years of blackouts and air raids, and the final battle of Berlin with Russian troops. This is also the story of how I met my husband, Ardell, and our struggle, through all of the red tape, for me to come to the United States so that we could be married.

My story, unlike some others, has a happy ending. Since coming to the United States so long ago, I have lived a full and happy life; but I will never forget the horrible days of the war. It is my hope that, with this book, I can offer people a glimpse into that time in history, and my experience can speak for so many others.

This is my story.

EDITH V. LANDIS

EDITH'S MOTHER, PAULINE, AND HER FATHER, WILLI

CHAPTER 1

My Childhood

I was born May 1, 1925, in Berlin, the capital city of Germany. My maiden name was Edith Vera Inge Quabeck. Willi, my father, died at the age of forty-four when I was just four months old. My mother, Pauline, raised me along with her four older children from a previous marriage. I had a very happy childhood. As far as I was concerned, Arthur, Paul, Grete, and Luzie were my brothers and sisters.

I was the youngest child by eleven years, and everyones' pride and joy. I had many friends, and I loved school and always got good grades. The teachers were strict, therefore every student tried to do their very best. The school was a few blocks away from where I lived. The girls were educated in one building and the boys in another.

The two buildings joined and shared a central courtyard. We were not allowed to mingle with the boys. I remember many times, in the winter, as we would leave school and pass the boys' schoolyard to get to the street, they would be waiting to bombard us with snowballs. The only time the boys and girls were together was when we had cause for special occasions. We had a large gymnasium in a separate building that was used on different days by the boys and the girls. It was equipped with everything needed for gymnastics.

I had some trouble with my music teacher, Miss Muller. Before chorus began, she would spray her mouth and throat with a yellow spray. One of my best friends, Ursula Witt, sat beside me and every time Miss Muller opened her mouth to sing, we couldn't help but start to giggle. She would stand right in front of us and when she opened her mouth to sing, all we could see was her yellow throat and tongue, and an occasional fine mist of yellow spray. Ursula would say, "We should have brought an umbrella!" No matter how often we were told to stop giggling, we just couldn't, and we never wanted to explain why we were laughing.

Finally, letters were sent home to our mothers requesting a meeting at the principal's office. The principal told my mother she was puzzled that I had gotten into trouble, because I had always been a very good student, and no teachers other than Miss Muller ever had any complaints about me. My mom replied that there was nothing she could do. When I think something is funny, and start laughing, I just cannot stop. I am like that to this day.

One day, after the war was over, I ran into Miss Muller on the street. We were both happy to see that the other had come through the war unharmed. She hoped that I could finally tell her why Ursula and I had those giggling spells in her class. I explained that we liked her as a teacher, but when she opened her mouth wide and we saw her yellow tongue, we couldn't help but giggle. Then I had to give her the bad news that Ursula had been killed a few days before the war ended. She had come out of her cellar to get some fresh air and, while she was standing in the doorway of her house, an artillery shell exploded in the middle of the street. Some of the fragments hit her in the stomach and killed her.

There was a big park, not far from our house, where we spent a lot of time playing. We also rode our bicycles on the sidewalks, and played in the courtyard behind the apartment house. In the summer we went swimming in the lakes. My mom and I lived in the same apartment house from the time I was born until I came to the United States. It was located in the center of Berlin. One side of our apartment house faced *Hermanplatz* — a big square, which was the center of six streets. To the other side was a block of apartment houses, including ours. Across the street was a large department store, *Karstadt,* which covered an entire block, and in between were the subways and bus stops.

Berlin was a beautiful city that was full of history. It had several rivers and lakes, lots of parks, and trees along the streets.

KARSTADT BEFORE THE WAR
I lived in the apartment building (far right) from birth until my departure from Germany.

BERLIN — TIERGARTEN
One of the many beautiful scenes in Germany before the war.

There were many churches, castles and museums that were hundreds of years old and built using various styles of architecture. There were opera houses, concert and dance halls, indoor and outdoor cafés, and nightclubs. Berlin possessed every type of activity and entertainment that you could want.

As I grew up, my siblings left home one by one. My brother, Paul, married and moved away. His wife's name was Frieda and they had two daughters, Brigitte and Monika. My second brother, Arthur, married twice. His first wife's name was Hedy and they had one son named Horst. Hedy died when Horst was a baby. Arthur's second wife was Meta, and together they had three children: Klaus, Hannelore, and Gert. Their family lived in the same apartment house that we did. My sister, Luzie, got married and she and her husband, Willi Ludley, had two sons, Manfred and Wolfgang. They also had a daughter, Hannelore, but she died as a baby. Luzie and her family lived in the same apartment house, too. My sister Grete never married. She was a ballet dancer and also played in the movies. When another little girl was needed for an occasional part, Grete took me to the movie set and I got the parts until I was twelve years old. Grete died of hepatitis in 1939 at the age of thirty-two.

CHAPTER 2

The Hitler Regime

In January 1933, Adolf Hitler came into power. During his regime, he referred to Germany as the *Third Reich,* and he wanted to be known as *Führer,* which means leader. He had organized the Nazi Party years before. The two major groups fighting against each other were the Communist Party and the Nazi Party.

There were two large beer halls up the street from my home. The Communists held their meetings on one side of the street and the Nazis on the opposite side. Many nights after their meetings, they would fight each other with fists, clubs and knives.

I remember when Hitler came into power, even though I was just seven and a half years old at the time. While I was at my girlfriend

Inge's house, it was announced over the radio. Most people were happy about it because, after World War I, Germany had been economically depleted. Jobs were scarce and the future was bleak for Germany's working class. When the German people seemed to have no hope left, Hitler became ruler, and promised better living conditions for everyone. Indeed, jobs became readily available, as did cheap vacations for the working class, and extra monetary benefits for each child. The future actually looked bright for the first few years after Hitler came into power.

It took little time for him to sway the young people over to his side. Thousands of teenagers, age fourteen and older, joined the *Hitler Youth*. The first few years, things seemed to be moving in the right direction. Children, from the age of ten to fourteen, joined organizations comparable to our Girl Scouts and Boy Scouts. The boys were called *Jungvolk* and the girls were called *Jungmädel*. Most of my friends and classmates joined the Jungmädel, as did I. We received training in honor, decency, truthfulness, independence, and pride. We went camping, did arts and crafts, and had a lot of training in sports. Hitler wanted to be sure we grew up strong and healthy. We had competitions, with girls from other areas, in track, relay racing, javelin throwing, and shot put. As children, we received good moral training, which, of course, impressed our parents. (How ironic it seems now. After all, how could someone so bad and so crazy teach children such good values? What a huge disappointment Hitler turned out to be.) Teenage girls, age fourteen and older, were called BDM, or *Bund Deutsher Mädels,* and they received the same basic training as the younger girls. Teenage boys, fourteen and older, were known as the *Hitler Youth*, and they advocated more radical training.

The so-called 'Nazis' were known as the *Sturm Abteilung* (Storm Troopers or SA), which Hitler organized before he came into power. This group wore brown uniforms with an armband around the left upper sleeve. The armband was red, with a white circle in the middle bearing a black *hakenkreutz* (swastika) in the center. Do not be misled by the name 'Storm Troopers.' They were not a military group, but were composed of people who were faithful followers of Hitler. They remained active until the start of the war, when they were drafted into the military like everyone else. They held big rallies, parades and social gatherings. Hitler's elite troops were known as the *Schutz Staffel* (SS), and they wore black uniforms. They were always ready for battle, and had to be in perfect physical condition. The

STORM TROOPER RALLY
Hitler's followers held many rallies, such as this one at the Brandenburg Gate, bearing torches and shouting support for their leader.

secret police were known as the *Gestapo*, and this was the group that everyone tried to avoid.

When the Gestapo arrested someone, they were usually never seen again. Next-door neighbors could not be trusted, because they could turn you in to the Gestapo for almost anything. If someone said something against Hitler or his regime, it was often repeated to the wrong person, then the Gestapo would be there to make an arrest.

The official name of Hitler's party was the *National Socialist German Workman's Party* (NSDAP). As far as the Party was concerned, it did not have much significance. Many people paid membership dues to the Party in order to keep their jobs. Before long everything began to change. It became common knowledge that anyone who spoke against Hitler or the government would be arrested. Hitler began to hate the Jews, who he blamed for controlling all the money. He forced them to wear the Star of David on their clothing.

I remember the nights of November 8th and 9th, 1938. This was later given the name *Kristallnacht*, or "Night of Broken Glass." The Storm Troopers held a rally, and smashed the windows out of stores belonging to Jews. They also burned synagogues and other Jewish properties. Of course, I can only speak of what happened in Berlin. There was only one Jewish family living in our apartment house, and they moved away.

In 1938, many Jewish professionals who had money, such as doctors and lawyers, left Germany and immigrated to other countries, like America and Australia. People were increasingly arrested — not only the Jews, as many people believed — and were sent to what became known as the Concentration Camps.

Hitler and his government officials convinced the people of Germany to believe that the concentration camps were like penitentiaries. However, people who were arrested and placed in the concentration camps were usually never seen again. I know it is difficult for Americans to believe that the German people did not know about the terrible things that were happening in the concentration camps, but it was all kept very secret. It is hard to believe that any human being could do such horrible things to other human beings. The German people were shocked and appalled when they witnessed the protrayal of World War II in the movies. No concentration camps were located near our home, so we hadn't the slightest idea of what had actually occurred in these prisons.

The Gestapo arrested those caught breaking the law in any way, or speaking out against Hitler and the Nazis. If we walked into a public office we had to say *"Heil Hitler."* Those who did not say it were immediately put on a 'black list' and watched by the secret police. For the next few years, if we were careful about what we said, and obeyed the law, our lives proceeded at a reasonable pace. I have to admit we did not have much crime during that time, because many of those arrested were never seen again. However, the people charged with crimes were never given a chance to prove their innocence.

One example of this happened to the son of my mother's friend. He was in his early thirties when he walked down the street past a grocery store on a hot summer day. He saw a little girl on the street crying for her mommy. He loved children, so he picked her up to console her. He was facing away from the store, and when the little girl's mother came running out looking for her, she saw him holding her little girl and screamed for the police. She accused him of trying to molest or kidnap her daughter, and the young man was arrested and sent to a concentration camp without a trial. A few months later, his mother received a telegram stating that he had died of a heart attack. We never believed this to be true, because he was a very healthy young man.

Another such incident happened on our street, involving a family consisting of a father, mother and five sons. The father received a deferment from the army, and worked in a war plant in Berlin, while all five sons served in the army. Three of the sons were killed in action, one was reported missing in action, and the youngest son was known to be somewhere in Russia. One morning, while the mother was having coffee with a friend, she received notification that her youngest son was missing in action. She threw her coffee cup at Hitler's picture on the wall and smashed it. She began speaking out against Hitler and calling him names. Her friend left the house and told someone. We are not sure whom she told, but in no time the Gestapo came and arrested the mother. When her husband came home from work and found out what had happened to his wife, he took a pistol and shot himself. He left a note stating that he had nothing left to live for. His sons were all gone and he knew, after the Gestapo arrested his wife, that he would never see her again.

I cannot emphasize enough how lucky the people of the United States are to have a democracy instead of a dictatorship. No matter how crazy it gets around election time, and regardless of who is elected President of the United States, that person does not have the power to force his will on other people, or have those killed who disagree with him. The President of the United States must always answer to the Senate, the House of Representatives and the people who elected him.

CHAPTER 3

World War Two – The Beginning

The school I attended was *18th Volksschule, Braunauer Strasse*. It was mandatory that we attended school for eight years. After completing eight years, we could either quit, pick a career and receive specialized training for three or four more years in that field, or go to college and become a professional such as a doctor or lawyer. I chose to attend business school and also learn the retail trade, so I went to school part-time while working in the textile department of Karstadt, one of the largest department stores in Berlin. After four years, I received my diploma and was qualified to open my own textile business.

In March 1939, I was confirmed in the Lutheran Church. I remember our minister telling us that we could pray in a closet, or think our prayers, and God would hear us. He said there was no need to shout and scream to God for help. I firmly believe that. Many times, when I was in danger, I believed God watched over me and answered my silent prayers.

World War II began on September 1, 1939, when I was fourteen years old. Hitler sent the German troops into Poland and other areas, with the reasoning that he wanted to re-claim the German territories that were taken during World War I. On September 3, 1939, England and France declared war on Germany. The conflict escalated. Hitler sent increasing numbers of troops all over Europe and North Africa. He would not heed the advice of his officers and advisors. Those who did not agree with him were executed.

Shortly after the war began, everything was rationed. Every three months we received ration books of stamps — one card for each month. Each card listed the time of day when we were permitted to get groceries — morning, noon or evening. It was all very organized. I do not remember the amounts we recieved because my mom would get the groceries while I was working. I do remember that we were allotted five pounds of potatoes per week for each person. Milk was only available for children, who received one pint per day.

There was always a long line of people waiting when the storekeeper received the supplies. Every month, the store owner had to paste each stamp that he received onto special paper, and send them to a certain office. This process made it impossible for a storekeeper to give more stamps to his family or friends. Everything had to be accounted for. I had this great fear that my mom would say something against Hitler while she was standing in line for groceries, and would be arrested.

Every year we received less, as shipping became almost impossible due to the destruction of transportation routes between the country and the city. Imports were cut off, as were luxury items like coffee, chocolate candy, nylon stockings, and much more. We became experts in making sandwiches out of anything. Between two pieces of bread and oleo, I would put slices of bananas (when we could get them), apples, cucumbers, onions, or mustard alone.

As the battles on land began, we received less and less food in Berlin. Most of the farms on the way to Berlin were being destroyed by artillery during the last and most bloody battle of the war. Toward the end of the war, we were lucky to have a slice of dry bread, or a few potatoes cooked in water with a little salt. Many times we stood

SCENE OF DESTRUCTION IN BERLIN

in line for potato rations, only to find that they had rotted before even reaching the store and would have to be thrown away. For a long period of time we didn't have vegetables, meat or fruit. Every six months we could ask for special authorized papers to get things other than food, such as articles of clothing, shoes, towels, and sheets.

When England declared war on Germany, the blackouts began. There was only one lighted pole, containing a blue bulb, on each city block. Automobiles were required to have blue headlights installed, and everyone had to pull their blinds down at night.

The streets at night were dark and still. It was very eerie to walk home after work. We could hear our footsteps echo through the bombed-out houses. We had to train our eyes to see in the dark after coming out of a lighted room. We were rarely afraid, however, because the crime rate was almost non-existent due to the consequences: those arrested were sent to the concentration camps.

There were many craters in the middle of streets from bomb explosions and it was difficult to move around. Sometimes we took chances hitch-hiking, and accepted rides from complete strangers. Everyone seemed like one great big family during that horrible war. Strangers were constantly helping strangers.

Each apartment house had an air raid shelter in the basement, furnished with army cots, bunk beds and chairs. We had sandbags outside the cellar windows so glass wouldn't hit us when shrapnel from the German anti-aircraft or bomb explosions broke the windows. The average apartment house was five to six stories high. Some buildings, such as *Karstadt,* were much higher.

There were public air raid shelters all over the city. The air raids began with one per night. Later, they escalated to several times a night. After the United States joined forces with England, the air raids occurred at any time. The sound of the air raid sirens filled our days and nights with terror. Bombs were falling and German anti-aircraft shrapnel was flying everywhere while the planes were being targeted.

We always went to bed at night fully dressed, except for our shoes and coats, so we could get to the shelters as quickly as possible when we heard the air raid sirens. Children were extremely terrified at night, and it was very difficult to wake them to go to the air raid shelters. It was especially painful to come out of the shelters and see the destruction that had occurred. Homes were completely destroyed, buildings were in rubble, and streets had huge craters in the middle of them from exploding bombs. Structures were burning

SCENE OF DESTRUCTION IN BERLIN

BERLINER AND FRENCH DOME BEFORE THE WAR

everywhere from the firebombs and many buildings were reduced to rubble. People were walking around crying and screaming because they lost their homes and all their belongings. Some even lost loved ones. There was chaos and destruction everywhere. This became the norm within our world.

BERLINER AND FRENCH DOME AFTER THE WAR

CHAPTER 4

Blackouts and Air Raids

The last year of the war, students had to go to school one hour each day. They met with their teachers in a large auditorium to get their daily homework, and to return it the next day. The older students had to be there from 8:00 to 9:00 a.m., and the younger ones from 9:00 to 10:00 a.m. Since all of the young men were drafted into the army, there was a shortage of teachers. To keep the educational system continuing as smoothly as possible, the government called retired teachers back to work. Of course, during the last few months of the war, there was no school at all. In April 1945, Berlin became a battlefield. Guns were given to every man, including retired teachers, to fight with the military.

The on-going terror brought the German people closer together. Everyone did their very best to help each other. Until the last year of the war, people continued to go to their jobs — that is, if the building was still standing. Gradually, all of the men were drafted, and only women and children remained in the shelters. Once the air raids became a daily occurrence, any women and children who had relatives in the country were encouraged to leave Berlin. Cities were the prime targets. At first, we would run across the street to a subway station upon hearing the air raid sirens, because we felt we had a better chance to escape. Unless a bomb hit us directly, we could walk through the tunnel and exit onto another street. We saw apartment houses bombed in our neighborhood, with sometimes as many as fifty people buried underneath.

When the air raids sounded, the current on the subway tracks was immediately turned off. The entrance to the subway was on *Hermanplatz*, across the street from us. There were two levels of tracks, an upper and a lower, and we would go to the lower level, jump on the tracks, and sit under a concrete ledge which was about five feet deep.

As we ran across the street, we could see the bombers in the beams of the German anti-aircraft searchlights, and the shrapnel from the anti-aircraft guns rained over us. People came from all directions with blankets and the one small suitcase that we all carried, which held precious belongings and basic necessities. While the German anti-aircraft guns were shooting at planes, the stairs of the subway station were so crowded with people that no one could fall down. It was total panic until everyone got down the stairs.

On one occasion during an air raid, we were down in the subway station with hundreds of other people, when we heard a little boy's voice calling my name. It sounded like my nephew Klaus, Arthur's son. We looked around and saw a little hand waving. We guessed right — it was Klaus! It was a miracle that we had heard him through all the noise. Arthur's wife Meta and their four children had been evacuated to a farm in East Germany, and were fortunate to catch the last train to Berlin before the Russian troops entered the area. We were so happy and relieved to see that Meta, Horst, Klaus, Hannelore and Gert were still alive.

Some of us had learned first aid and fire fighter training, though not much could be done when firebombs were thrown. These bombs were filled with a phosphorous gas which splattered and could not be extinguished with water, but rather had to be smothered with sand. To be prepared if the need arose, everyone kept several buckets of sand in their apartments.

In spite of being scared much of time, we young people still managed to find plenty of things to laugh about. For instance, during one memorable air raid while we were hiding in the subway station, we jumped down on the tracks after the current had been turned off, and sat under a concrete ledge for added protection. Suddenly, a bomb hit a different entrance to the subway and the air from the impact blew through the tunnel so fast that we had to sit hunched over with our heads down. When it was over, and we could lift our heads, I saw that a black, soot-like substance from the tracks had blown through and settled all around us. I looked at my mom and started laughing. Her face was all black, and her hat was standing straight up because she had fastened it with a rubber band around the back of her hair. She was very upset with me for finding this funny after such a scare. When I told her why I was laughing, she looked at me and told me that my face was also black with soot, and so was the face of everyone else. I suppose one is conditioned to keep going while living through six years of war. If we didn't laugh we would lose our minds.

We tried to keep our spirits up, and hoped from day to day that the nightmare would end. We also tried to be cheerful in front of the children and the elderly. I remember daydreaming with friends how nice it would be after the war ended. We could have a good cup of coffee, or maybe some chocolate candy, go to bed with a good book, and everything would be peaceful again. But, much to our dismay, that was not to be for a very long time.

In March of 1943, while we were once again standing in the subway during an air raid, we could hear planes above us and bombs exploding around us. Someone yelled from the outside that our house was on fire. Before my family realized what was happening, I dashed outside to take a look. I saw that the roof above our apartment, and my sister's apartment, was on fire, so I ran inside and up the stairs to check out the damage. Substance from a firebomb had splattered on the couch and was smoldering on the floor. I smothered it with sand, hoping to prevent it from damaging the floor and burning through to the apartment below. A friend of mine called for me and came up to help. He and I tossed our smoldering couch through a window on the fifth floor. As soon as it hit the air, the couch became engulfed in a big ball of flames. Thank God — only one room was ruined at that time. Meanwhile, the air raid ended and I realized that people were watching me. My family was petrified when they saw me on the fifth floor directly below the burning roof.

Several times I was close to being hurt or killed, but during those moments I was never very scared. It is amazing what a person can accomplish in a life or death situation.

We teenagers, many of us, were very busy in those years, helping wherever and whenever we were needed. Once, when firebombs hit the house next door, a few of us ran up to get some belongings out of an apartment. I was coming out the back door, holding a heavy box in my arms, and someone screamed. Startled, I took a quick step backwards. At that moment, a burning log fell down from the roof and landed in the spot where I had been standing a second before. Lucky for me, someone saw the burning log falling and warned me. It surely could have killed me!

Until the last two years of the war, and in spite of the air raids, we teenagers lived as normally as possible. I had many friends, both male and female. We would go on dates to theaters, movies, or cafés, and listen to music. Dancing was not allowed while German soldiers were at the battlefront. When the air raid siren sounded, we all ran to the nearest shelter; and when it was over, we continued what we were doing. As long as we kept our tickets, we could return to the theaters and stay to see the rest of the show. We always remained close to home so that we would know that our families were safe after an air raid.

There was one famous ballroom dance school in Berlin. It was called *Tanzschule Keller*. It was allowed to operate during the first few months of the war. One day the owner of the dance school came to Karstadt, where I was working while attending business school. He asked my boss if he would recommend a few nice girls for lessons. The lessons would be free, for a lot of young German soldiers who were stationed in Berlin had enrolled, but there were not enough young ladies for partners. My boss asked me if I would be interested, and since there was no dancing allowed anywhere else, I gladly accepted. It was a lot of fun and I learned all the ballroom dances, such as the Tango, Fox Trot, Waltz, Rumba, Cha Cha, Mambo and Samba. The course lasted three months. We had lessons twice a week, from 8:00 to 10:00 p.m. When the lessons ended, the school held a big Gala Ball for us, complete with a grand orchestra. There was a dance competition for the Waltz, Tango and Fox Trot. The soldiers wore their uniforms and the girls wore long gowns. My gown was made of a light-green, satin fabric, and was very festive. My partner and I won second place in the dance competition! We each received flowers and a certificate. After the Gala Ball, all the dance schools were closed until the end of the war.

In the summer, we went to the lakes outside Berlin to swim. If the air raid sirens blasted, we would hurry out of the water, away from the beach, and run into the nearby woods. From there, we could see the planes flying to Berlin, but figured they would not waste their bombs on a bunch of trees. In the city during an air raid, we could see the planes above and the German anti-aircraft shooting at them. Of course, shrapnel from the German anti-aircraft would be flying around, so it was important to get off the streets as soon as possible.

CHAPTER 5

The Job

In 1943, after I graduated from Business School, the German army began drafting women into service. At the time, I was working in Karstadt, the department store across the street from where I lived. One day a friend of mine stopped to tell me that she had acquired a job at the German Army Headquarters in Berlin, and therefore would not have to go into service with the armed forces. She suggested that I try to get a job there as well.

I went for an interview and was hired after passing the test. I was not quite eighteen years of age at the time. By working within the German Army Headquarters, I could remain a civilian and go home to my family after each shift. I was placed in the Communications

Center, where we received and transmitted communications for the German troops from all over Europe. It was very interesting work. Since most of the positions were filled by German soldiers and officers, there were only a few civilian women hired, and we worked the swing shifts.

During the night shift, we often connected the soldiers at the frontline, or wherever they were stationed in Europe, with their families in Germany. They always had to go through our switchboard. It was a very interesting job, and I loved it. Of course, the calls were free of charge for the soldiers. Many times the soldiers wanted to chat with us for awhile after they talked to their loved ones at home. It was a lot of fun. After our shift we'd usually have to walk home, which would take an hour or more. Occasionally, we would catch a ride with someone part of the way. Because of the damage caused by the air raids, the subways and buses were no longer running.

With the passing of each year, the struggles of daily existence became harder for the German civilians. I suppose the strategy of the Allies was to break the morale and spirit of the German soldiers by destroying their families and homes. The problem with this strategy was the attitude of the power-crazy ruler, *Adolf Hitler*. It made no difference to him how many women and children died, or to what extent Germany was destroyed. Any soldier, officer or advisor who objected to his plans was killed. He would not stop the madness.

The German troops were sent to the *'Battle of Stalingrad'* late in 1942. It was the biggest battle in Russia. It was bitter cold, and no German supplies could reach the desperate troops. Still, Hitler would not give up. He sent more and more German soldiers into battle.

I remember the sad day in February 1943 when the German National Anthem was playing over the radio. It was announced that the Russians took Stalingrad, and thousands of German soldiers had died or were taken prisoner. We cried for all those young men, but we didn't realize at the time that my brother, Arthur, was in that battle. We still don't know what happened to him. He was reported missing at the age of twenty-eight. In the last letter we received from him, he wrote that he had been in a field hospital for a short time with frostbite on his hands and feet, but was back with his unit again. He said that food and supplies had not gotten through for a while. Then, at the end of the letter, Arthur wrote that he could hear German planes, which hopefully meant supplies were arriving. Later, I learned that some planes did get through, rescuing a few wounded soldiers, along with some mail, before they were all completely surrounded by the Russian Army. Arthur never received the telegram informing him of the birth of his youngest son, Gert.

After the war was over, some German soldiers returned home from prison camps. Gert was about two and a half years old, and he only knew his dad from photographs. A few times he came running to his mom, saying "Mama, papa is coming home!" Each time we looked, hoping it was Arthur. It always turned out to be a stranger, walking by in a German Army uniform. The soldiers' uniforms were tattered, and their boots were worn out from walking hundreds of miles. A few soldiers even wore rags on their sore, swollen feet. The majority of them were physically and mentally crushed. My brother Arthur never came home.

CHAPTER 6

The Assassination Attempt

Several attempts were made to assassinate Hitler, but each time he managed to get away with only a few scratches. The last attempt was made just before midnight on July 20, 1944. I remember working the night shift at headquarters. We received a call stating that Hitler was assassinated, and another officer would be taking command. This new leader planned to stop the nightmare and surrender to the allies. A few minutes later, all hell broke loose. Hitler called on his private line, screaming that he was still in command.

Apparently, during a meeting inside Hitler's Headquarters, *Wolfschanze*, near a little town in East Prussia, there was an attempt to assassinate him. Oberst von Stauffenberg, who was one of his officers,

HITLER ASSASSINATION ATTEMPT
One of Adolf Hitler's officers reportedly placed a briefcase containing explosives under a table near Hitler in a failed attempt to assassinate him, according to this article.

placed a bomb-filled briefcase at Hitler's feet. The briefcase was accidentally pushed aside, and when the bomb was detonated, Hitler was not seriously injured, and received only minor cuts and scratches. It was a terrible night at the communications center. We did not know what would happen next. Hitler was constantly on the phone. He was on a rampage. There was so much confusion.

In the meantime, seven of the officers involved, including Oberst von Stauffenberg, came to our communication headquarters in Berlin. Hitler's SS guards immediately replaced the Army guards at the gates. During that night, they chased down and shot all seven of the officers, and threw them on trucks like cattle.

The chauffeur of General Olbricht, one of the officers who had been shot, had asked me out on dates several times, but I never accepted. He had given me the general's telephone number, where I could reach him if I ever needed a ride home after work. I kept the general's telephone number in my notebook. The next morning, when the girls from dayshift came in to relieve us, they told us that the former Army guards at the gates had been replaced by SS guards, and they were checking everything in pockets and purses. If they suspected anyone of having knowledge of the assassination, or a connection to the officers involved, they would arrest them.

I swear that God must have been watching over me, or I was blessed with a guardian angel during that horrible war. At the last minute, before I left work and went through the gate, I remembered that the general's telephone number was in my notebook. I went into the bathroom, tore out the page, and flushed it down the toilet. Sure enough, at the gate, the SS guards searched through my belongings, including my notebook. Ten thousand people all over Germany were suspected and placed under arrest. Thousands were executed, and I could have been one of them. I never saw the general's chauffeur again after that night.

The incident had been announced over the German radio, and my family was frantic with worry. They didn't know if I was all right, because no specific details had been given. They tried to contact me, but calls from local phones were not accepted. My family, and the families of the other workers, had to wait until we got home to know that we were safe.

The madness of Hitler continued. Germany was becoming completely devastated. What hadn't been destroyed by bombs was hit by artillery from the American troops in the west, and Russian troops in the east. We didn't know it at the time, but the American troops stopped at the Elbe River and decided to let the Russians fight the battle for Berlin.

On April 15, 1945, the army doctor gave me sick leave because I had bronchitis, a high fever, and difficulty breathing. He prescribed me medicine and I soon recovered, but still couldn't return to work. Once again, I felt that God was looking after me, because, instead of working at the Communication Center, I was home with my family during the final battle of Berlin.

On April 20, 1945, the sky in the distance was red with artillery fire. We could no longer take the chance to run across the street to the subway station. Instead, we all stayed in the basement air raid shelter of our apartment house. There were forty-six adults and sixteen children. There was no electricity, and candlelight was the only light we had. We could hear the continuous shooting of artillery in the distance. It gradually came closer and closer.

I was nineteen at the time and my girlfriend, Gerda, was seventeen. At night, Gerda and I slept side by side on two armchairs that we pushed together. If one of us wanted to turn, we both had to turn. We could not leave the basement for any reason. The Germans and Russians were shooting at each other and we were caught in the middle of their artillery.

We remained in the basement during air raids, and when the artillery was shooting outside. It was terrible and very frightening, because we never knew what would happen next. To calm the children and the elderly, a few of us would sing songs to distract them from the noise and explosions outside. It was very difficult to pretend that everything was normal, when on the inside we were just as scared as they were.

The conditions were very poor in our basement shelter. We had taken water down in the beginning, but there was little left to drink. There was no extra water for washing or taking baths. We wore the same dirty clothes for weeks at a time.

Down the hall there was a portable toilet, and the pungent odor gradually traveled throughout the basement. It was unbearable. A few times, Gerda and I took a chance and ran up to the second floor toilet. The artillery would stop for a few moments when the soldiers reloaded their guns. Each time the artillery stopped and I pulled my pants down to use the toilet, the shooting would start again and I'd have to pull my pants back up. This happened several times. Like a couple of fools, we started laughing. Gerda said I should just go ahead and finish. I replied that I didn't want to be found with my pants down if Russian shrapnel hit us! Finally, I finished my business. It is odd, but we teenagers could find something funny in even the grimmest situations.

After the war ended, I saw women walking down the street

with evidence of head lice. They may have been in hiding for a longer period of time. Areas had been set up to treat those infected, but we could see that nits were still evident on many of them.

CHAPTER 7

The Battle of Berlin

On May 1, 1945, my twentieth birthday, a friend of mine, Dora Schultz, woke me up while I was dozing. She had written a beautiful poem for me, and threw it on my face. It was her birthday gift to me. The poem doesn't rhyme in its English translation, but gives you an idea of people's thoughts on the war.

> *Candles burn in our circle*
> *but not to celebrate your birthday*
> *Because the times are too sad*
> *for us adults and the children*
> *Sorrow lives in our hearts*

So by the light of the cellar candles

you have to spend this day instead

to celebrate and sing

But it has to change someday

Our misfortune and terror will end

The sun will shine for us again

and we don't have to cry anymore

The youth can laugh again

Children can play

The old ones can relax again

and we all will live in peace again

Here by the light of the cellar candles

I wish you from the bottom of my heart

Stay healthy, keep your courage

and everything will be good for you again

The German artillery and tanks were now positioned in front of our apartment building, and the Soviets were firing towards them. Suddenly, the Soviet artillery hit our building and knocked down six apartments. Judging by the way everything shook, we thought the

KARSTADT ON THE LAST DAY OF THE WAR — MAY 1, 1945
A few hours later, Russian Troops occupied this street and the entire area in which we lived.

entire building was being demolished, and we feared we would be buried alive. Thank God that was not the case. However, the artillery fire had destroyed two apartments on the third floor, two apartments on the fourth floor, and two apartments on the fifth floor — those belonging to my sister, and my mom and me. We lost everything.

Later that day, two German soldiers came into our shelter to tell us that they had orders to dynamite Karstadt, the department store across the street from us. It was burning at one end and there was no time to fight the fire because the building was an entire city block wide. The soldiers allowed anyone willing to brave the artillery fire to run across the street to Karstadt and get whatever they wanted. Since the majority of people living in our apartment house were elderly and small children, Gerda and I decided to take the chance. She and I were always volunteering for things, because we could run faster than everyone else.

We could hear constant shooting in the distance, but there was always a pause when the artillery guns were being reloaded in the area around our apartment. We listened for this pause, and, when we felt it was safe, we sprinted across the street to Karstadt. We grabbed a clothesbasket that we could fill with food from the grocery department. The only items left were sugar, raisins, almonds and a few crackers. While we were still in the building, the artillery fire began again. Two German soldiers came running into the store and told us that many people had been wounded or killed outside. The Russians started shooting at them as they were running to and from the store. The German soldiers stayed with Gerda and me until the shooting stopped. Then they carried our basket across the street to our basement shelter.

It was a nightmare when we stepped outside. People were lying all over the square, and it looked as if everyone was dead. The soldiers would not let us stop and look because, as soon as we were across the street, the shrapnel started flying again. There were people trapped inside Karstadt who wouldn't or couldn't leave. The building was soon blown up and many of those people died inside.

Later, soldiers brought an elderly woman into our shelter for me to attend to. Her face and body were covered in blood from shrapnel wounds. One of her legs was just barely hanging on below the knee. Trying to stop the bleeding was the only thing I could do; but, as I took her pulse, I noticed that she was already dead. The soldiers also checked her pulse and confirmed my findings. A law stated that we were not allowed to keep the dead in our homes because of disease, so the soldiers took the woman's body outside and placed it with the others on the street to be later identified by relatives.

Near the end of the war, every male was given a gun and expected to fight. Boys fourteen and older who belonged to the Hitler Youth, and even old men, were sent into combat.

A few days before the end of the war, a friend of mine from headquarters came on motorcycle looking for me. He was on patrol for his unit and stopped to tell me that the Russians were fighting in Berlin. He said I should be in hiding, because he heard that they were very cruel to women, and were raping them along the way.

The night of May 1, 1945, while we were still hiding in the cellar, we heard shoveling and what sounded like guns being thrown down. We didn't know if the German soldiers were leaving, or if the Russians had come to set the apartment house on fire. The entrance to our cellar was in the back courtyard, through a set of double iron doors that lifted up. Once inside, our shelter was located a couple of hallways back from this door.

At one point that night, we heard heavy footsteps outside, coming right up to the cellar door. It was very scary. Whoever was there never tried to come in. The Russians took our street that night, and we never knew if it had been German soldiers checking things out before they left, or Russian soldiers who didn't trust to open the door. The next morning at daybreak we could only hear shooting in the distance.

Heinz, a man that lived in our house, had deserted his unit a few days before and returned home to be with his family. He decided to sneak out early that morning to see what was happening. When he came back, he told us that he had tried to open one of the apartment house doors that led to the street, but it wouldn't give until he forced it. He then discovered that somebody had propped the dead woman, the one I had tended to earlier, against the door. We wondered if German soldiers had placed her there to mislead the Russians into thinking that everyone was dead, or if the Russians had done it for some reason. Heinz also reported that he'd seen tanks across the street. The way they were positioned, he could only see some of the big white letters. He wasn't sure if they spelled USA or USSR. Unfortunately, it turned out to be USSR (Russia), as my friend from headquarters had warned me.

CHAPTER 8

The Russian Occupation

Several German men, who had been silent communist sympathizers, suddenly emerged like bugs out of the woodwork and appointed themselves in charge. Thank goodness there was only a handful of them. A frightened old man who lived in our apartment house went to the Russian soldiers and told them he was a communist. He then told us that the Russians were on our street and, if we put a white handkerchief around our arm, we could go across the street to Karstadt to get water. We could no longer get water in our apartments, but the waterline was still working over there. Gerda and I, along with others from the area, each took two buckets and went across the street.

Russian tanks were everywhere and the soldiers were busy bandaging their wounded comrades. One of the soldiers approached, asking the German name for water. When I replied "wasser," he smiled and let me go. I mentioned to Gerda that the Russians didn't seem as cruel as Hitler made them out to be. It had probably just been more of his propaganda.

We had to stand in line for a while to get water. When we came out, several Russian soldiers, including the one that had asked me about the water, were standing by the gate taking jewelry from people. I had on a gold watch and ring, but the soldier who had spoken to me simply smiled, and motioned for me to keep going. As soon as I got back to our cellar, I hid all of my valuables. Later, however, I had to trade those items for food.

The first Russian troops to fight in Berlin consisted mostly of Mongolians, who were very unkempt and sloppy. They had Asian features, and many of them wore ugly mustaches which hung down on the sides. They were also very cruel. It seemed as if they had been raised in the back woods or Russian mountains. They didn't appear to be educated, and acted like they had never seen normal women or modern gadgets. A group of them destroyed a bathroom and said

"German pigs have toilet in house!" They were just as happy to steal cheap costume jewelry, like brightly colored beads, as they were to steal fine, expensive jewelry. They took everything. They were very uncivilized and ignorant.

I was told, after things settled down, that one day a Russian soldier went to a German watchmaker. He had an alarm clock, and he gave the watchmaker cigarettes and said, "Take this clock and make two watches out of it. You have enough pieces here." The German man thought that, if the Russian was that stupid, he would take the cigarettes and say that he would try. I never heard how the story ended.

The Russian units were constantly being replaced by other units. At the beginning of their occupation, some high-ranking officers, who were not Mongolian, set up headquarters in a restaurant across the street from us. Since they were in our area of the city, the soldiers acted fairly decent.

On the night of May 2, 1945, after Berlin surrendered to the Russians and the fighting ended, the Russian soldiers got drunk and celebrated. While we hid in the cellar, we listened to them dancing and singing in the streets. Later, we could hear them smashing in doors, and the sounds of women screaming in the side streets. This continued for several weeks. Night and day the Russian soldiers raped women, including several of my friends. Those who resisted were killed. One of my friends was found in a doorway. After she was raped, her head had been smashed in with a rifle butt.

One of my friends was married to a German soldier who was missing in action. She and her father were going from the cellar to their apartment one day, when three Russian soldiers followed them. They were drunk and wanted my friend to go with them. Her father knew what they intended to do, so he stood in front of her and said, "You are not taking my girl." One of the soldiers pulled out his pistol and shot him. They would not let his daughter help him, and he bled to death as they took her away and raped her.

There is also the story of a young woman with two daughters, ages three and nine years old. Several Russian soldiers raped the mother and her nine-year-old daughter. After the incident, she gave poison to her two little girls and then took some herself. She left a note saying that she didn't want her children to go through that kind of hell ever again. After the war, we saw the husband visiting the cemetery where his wife and daughters were buried.

We were lucky to have the Russian headquarters located across the street from us. No one in our house had been raped or hurt. Only two soldiers had ever visited our cellar. When we heard their footsteps, Gerda and I quickly slid under an army cot and lay motionless on a blanket on the concrete floor. Gerda's mother placed the children on the cot and pushed things in front to hide us. The place was so crowded that it was difficult for anybody to look under the cot.

One of the soldiers sat down on a chair right in front of us. From where I lay hiding, I could see his boots, and thought that, at any moment, he would surely hear me breathing. I had heard the screams of women who were raped, and I was terrified that I might suffer the same fate. Luckily, he happened to be a nice man who could speak some German. He talked to the children, and I heard him say that he was a schoolteacher in Moscow. The other soldier was not so nice. He was busy stealing from everyone, and took whatever he wanted before they finally left.

Beginning the first day of the Russian occupation, we had a curfew from 9:00 p.m. through 5:00 a.m. Guards were stationed at the crossroads in front of our house, and they shot any German who went outside during that time. The curfew was strictly enforced.

By the beginning of May, my sister was eight months pregnant and due to have her baby at any time. We heard that we could obtain a permit from Russian headquarters permitting us to be on the street during curfew hours to go to the hospital if necessary. I went across the street to the headquarters and requested a permit. It was no use. I was told that they didn't care what happened. My sister would just have to manage until the curfew ended at 5:00 a.m.

It just so happened that her water broke and the labor pains started shortly before 5:00 a.m. There was no public transportation and everything was in ruins, so I decided to put my sister in a wagon and pull her. We left just after 5:00 a.m., and I managed to pull her six blocks to the hospital, over rubble from burned-out, artillery-damaged buildings. She gave birth to a baby girl and named her Hannelore, after my brother Arthur's daughter.

Since my sister had been under tremendous stress during her pregnancy and had received little nourishment, she was in poor condition. The baby was very small and weak as well, and it was not possible for my sister to nurse her. No one could buy milk or formula, and it was even difficult for the hospital to receive supplies. After a few weeks in the hospital, baby Hannelore died.

I will never forget the day we buried Hannelore. We found a small white wooden box. At the hospital, they wrapped the baby in some blankets and placed her in the little box. Since the cemetery down the street from us was filled (there were bodies from the battle still lying on top of the ground), we had to take the baby to another cemetery quite a distance away. My sister and I put the tiny casket in the wagon, and traveled with it up and down embankments, over railroad tracks and more rubble. When we finally reached our destination, I checked to be sure the baby's body hadn't bounced around too much. I opened the lid and arranged her in a proper position. I will never forget it. That poor little baby reminded me of a tiny bird with its mouth partly open. We could tell she had starved to death and no doubt had experienced other complications as well. It was utterly heart breaking.

One evening we looked out the window, just a few minutes before the 9:00 p.m. curfew, and saw a young German soldier standing on the corner. He looked to be seventeen or eighteen years old, and his uniform was torn, his boots were tattered. He seemed confused and didn't move from that spot. I knew that, when the Russian guards came out at 9:00 p.m. for curfew and saw him standing there, they would shoot him. I ran down to warn him, to tell him that he needed to get off the street, however, I noticed immediately that something was wrong with him. He appeared to be shell-shocked and refused to leave. He told me that he had received orders from his commanding officer not to leave his post. He had to remain there until he received further notice.

By now, curfew was fast approaching and the shelter was two blocks away. I had to think quickly! I told him that I, myself, had just spoken to his commanding officer, and was given orders to take him to a certain location to report for duty. It worked, and he came with me! Of course, I took him directly to the shelter. I ran all the way home and made it just in time for curfew. It was very frightening once the Russian guards came out at 9:00 p.m. to set up watch from the crossroads. If any Germans broke curfew, they were shot.

Later, everyone came out of the cellar and returned to their apartments. Since my sister, her two boys, my mom, and I had lost our apartments by artillery, we were assigned another apartment in the same building. It had once been a dentist's office.

A few days after the Russian takeover, thousands of German prisoners were marched through our street to another destination. At this point, we had no choice but to travel approximately five blocks to a brewery for our water. On the way back, we couldn't cross the street until all the German prisoners, flanked by Russian guards, passed by. I did not realize at the time that most of my friends from headquarters had been among those prisoners. The poor men looked so exhausted, and some were wounded and wearing bandages. I saw that most of them had cups or canteens hanging from their belts, so I made sure to place my buckets of water close to the curb. Several prisoners soon dipped into the buckets to get a drink. A Russian guard noticed, and spitefully kicked over the buckets, spilling all of the water out onto the ground. Suddenly, I lost my temper and just didn't care what might happen to me. I yelled at him in German, telling him what I thought of his cruel behavior. I'm sure he didn't understand a word I'd said, but he had seen the expression on my face. The guard pointed his rifle at me, said something in Russian, and cocked it ready to pull the trigger. I thought surely it was the end for me. But, once again, something unexpected happened. I didn't know that, while I was waiting to cross the street, a high-ranking Russian officer was also waiting to cross the street. When he saw what the Russian guard was about to do, he stepped beside me and reprimanded the guard, who then put his rifle down and marched on.

The following day, a German woman came to my house and gave me a note. She said one of the German soldiers dropped it on the street while passing her house. She had immediately placed her foot on the note so the guards wouldn't see it, then picked it up after they had passed. The note bore my name and address, and it was from a friend of mine named Reinhard. He asked me to locate his aunt in Berlin and tell her that he was taken prisoner. She could then notify his parents and inform them of what had happened to him.

As it turned out, the Russians took all the prisoners to Siberia, even after the war was over. A friend of mine found me in July of 1946, and told me that he had been among those prisoners. Because he was very sick, the Russians had released him, which was highly unusual. This friend went on to tell me that he had seen Reinhard performing very hard labor in a Siberian prison camp. He was not permitted to speak to him, but said that he appeared to be in very bad shape. I don't think Reinhard, like so many others, came out of prison alive. I'm sure he would have contacted me if he had.

I also heard that all the girls I worked with at headquarters, who couldn't get away, were taken prisoner. Some were raped and some were killed, and I never saw or heard from any of them. Once again, I had been spared. I was home with my family at the time, placed on sick leave for bronchitis and fever.

The whole city was a confusing, chaotic mess. There were burned and shot-out houses everywhere. People, mostly women and children, were aimlessly walking around with nowhere to go. A few shelters were kept open in beer halls and other public buildings that had not been completely distroyed. Notes to loved ones were placed

POSTED NOTES TO LOVED ONES

KURFURSTENDAMM IN THE YEAR 1945

everywhere around the ruins so those who were fortunate enough to survive the war could find each other.

The first few weeks after the Russians took Berlin, they made us clear the rubble from the streets so their vehicles could pass. We also had to clean up the rubble from the destruction of Karstadt. Bricks had to be cleaned and neatly stacked.

One night shortly before the nine o'clock curfew, my brother Paul's wife, Freida, and her daughters, Brigitte and Monika, came looking for us. They had been evacuated to a farm in East Germany during the latter part of the war. While the Russians fought their way toward Berlin, they acted like animals to the civilians wherever they passed through. My sister-in-law told us that she and the girls — Brigitte, nine years old, and Monika, one year old — had been hiding with other women and children in a barn, and when they thought that the Russian soldiers had passed, had gone back into the farmhouse to get some belongings. They didn't realize that several soldiers were still in the house. The soldiers sent the two little girls outside while they raped Freida.

When the war was over, she took a stroller and her two girls and began walking to Berlin, hoping that they would still have a home when they arrived. They spent many weeks traveling, and sometimes along the way, farmers would allow them to sleep in their barns for the night. When they reached Berlin, they found the house they had lived in was nothing but a pile of debris. So they walked to our house and we shared our apartment with them.

CHAPTER 9

German Soldiers Return Home

Slowly, one by one, German soldiers came home with torn uniforms and rags on their feet, completely exhausted and sick. It was heartbreaking to witness. They must have walked hundreds of miles. I think many of them came from English or American prison camps, because the Russians sent prisoners captured in Berlin during the last days of the war to Siberia. Those prisoners didn't come home for a long time, if they were lucky enough to come home at all.

It still upsets me to hear news commentators, and others in America, referring to World War II Germany as "Nazi Germany," and the German soldiers as "Nazis." Nothing is further from the truth. Most of the young men were drafted just like the young men from other countries. They were very brave, and fought for Germany, not for Hitler. War is hell. When I witnessed German soldiers coming home one by one, physically and emotionally destroyed by the actions of a crazy, fanatical ruler, it was heartwrenching. If only all of the rulers of the world, who sit behind desks ordering young men into battle, would settle differences amongst themselves; then no one would have to experience the horrors of war. The German soldiers had no choice. In the end, it was a matter of survival — to kill or be killed. I am sure that the average soldier, on either side, would prefer not to kill another human being. There will always be a few sadistic men who don't mind the killing. Thank God there are not too many of them in this world.

CHAPTER 10

The American Occupation

In July 1945, the allies decided to divide Berlin into four sectors, since it was the capital city of Germany. The West side was occupied by troops from England, France and America; while the East side was occupied by troops from Russia. Thank God, the district in which we lived was occupied by American troops.

I'll never forget the day the Russian troops left Berlin. It was such a relief. During the daytime hours, more and more Russian units passed through the streets on their way from German farms. They traveled in hay wagons pulled by cows. The wagons were loaded with things they had stolen — furniture, feather ticks, pillows — everything imaginable.

I remember one incident in particular. One of the cows that was pulling a heavy wagon kept falling down. The Russian driver of the wagon beat the cow repeatedly to make it stand up. After several attempts the cow could not get up, so the Russian shot it and left it there in the street.

Since we couldn't get much food, other than a little bread and a few potatoes, it took just a few minutes for a dozen or so Germans to come running with knives and butcher the dead cow right there in the street. Everyone took a piece of meat. I watched through the window but refused to take part. There was so much commotion and, furthermore, I didn't trust to eat the meat. The cow may have been diseased, and after getting so far without being killed, I surely didn't want to die of food poisoning!

A bakery was located just across the street from our apartment. Every day they received a certain amount of flour to bake fresh bread. We would wait inside our house until 5:00 a.m., then run across the street to stand in line for a loaf of bread. Usually, we shared it with others who couldn't get to the bakery before the bread was gone. One of our German neighbors later wrote me in America to tell me she never forgot the time that I shared my last slice of bread with her. To me, it was merely a natural thing to do. I would never have considered eating the entire slice in front of her without sharing it.

The arrival of the American troops was like a breath of fresh air. They appeared very neat, but we weren't sure how they would treat us. We heard from some of the German soldiers, who made it home from American prison camps, that they had been treated well. We could go about our daily routine without being afraid, and I never heard any report of physical violence. I suppose their worst behavior was flirting after having a few drinks. When they noticed a girl walking by, their favorite saying was "Hello baby!" No girls, that I knew of, were ever molested by an Amerian soldier.

When the American occupation troops came to our part of the city, the curfew was extended from 9:00 p.m. to 11:00 p.m. There were no more armed guards at the crossroads. Since we were free to go where we wished, we discovered a new way to get food. A few friends and neighbors would walk with me to the railroad depot about thirty minutes away. By the time we got there, the train was usually filled with passengers. Sometimes we stood on the running boards, and other times we climbed to the top of the train. We'd lie flat on our stomachs while holding on to anything we could find. It was very dangerous to lay on top of the trains. Once, a young man sat up while facing the back of the train. Suddenly, the train came to a halt, and there was a lot of commotion. We were told that the young man's head was cut off as the train went through an underpass.

In the country, we would get off the train and walk for miles from farm to farm, begging for potatoes or anything else to eat. In the beginning, the farmers would trade a few potatoes for items such as sweaters. But soon they had no more food to give, because so many city people were traveling to their farms. Once or twice we passed apple trees, and helped ourselves to the fruit.

During the latter part of 1945 and 1946, 'black market' business was commonly conducted. Only the people who had a lot of money, or something to trade, could do business. There were no places for Germans to buy cigarettes, so Americans could sell a pack for ten dollars. Candy bars and nylon stockings were also very popular items.

After the war, the people of Berlin who lived in the American sector hauled all of the rubble to four big parks. In each park, they made a high mountain of debris and covered it with topsoil. They then planted trees, shrubs, and flowers. It took a few years to complete and the result was beautiful.

CHAPTER 11

A Match Made in Heaven

On September 26, 1945, I met my future husband. It all started when my friend Lotti located me. She'd been drafted into the *Blitzmädel* (Air Force Communications), and had just returned home the previous day. When she saw our apartment had been shot out, she feared we might have been killed. After doing some investigating, she was told where to find me. It was a nice, sunny day, and we went for a walk to catch up on everything that had happened during the past year.

We walked down Hasenheide Street and came upon a little café. Music was pouring out and people were dancing. She suggested we go in and sit down. At first I was not too keen on the idea, because the place was packed with Germans and American soldiers. As soon as we walked in, an American soldier jumped up and asked us to sit at a table with him and his buddy. He could speak German and I told him no, thank you, we would find our own table. He insisted that there were no other seats available, and after looking around and realizing he was right, we accepted his invitation.

The soldier's name was Charlie and he introduced us to his buddy, whose name was Ardell. His nickname was "Tom" because "Ardell" was too difficult for Germans to pronounce. Charlie asked me to dance quite often, and Ardell sat quietly with Lotti, watching the two of us dance.

Lotti and I went to the ladies room where she told me that she was getting bored because Ardell did not even attempt a conversation with her. He was constantly watching Charlie and I dance, and she was ready to leave. When we returned to the table, Charlie and Ardell were having a serious discussion that we didn't understand. Later, when I was again dancing with Charlie, he told me that Ardell was very attracted to me, as was he, and that I must decide which of the two I preferred walk me home. I told him that I lived just down the street and didn't actually need *anybody* to walk me home, however, I did think that Ardell was very nice. He was quiet and reserved and I liked that. We later left the café as a foursome, all walking down the street together.

Charlie and Lottie, and Ardell and I, made a date for the next evening. I didn't intend to keep the date because I believed they would not show up, and I really wasn't keen on getting involved with an American soldier. However, the next day, Lotti picked me up for our double date, and so began a beautiful friendship.

Since I spoke very few English words, and Ardell spoke very few German, we took Charlie along on our dates. After about a month, I understood the majority of what Ardell was saying, and he understood me, though we each couldn't speak the other's language very proficiently.

He talked a lot about his family, and showed me photographs of them. His parents were Lester L. and Melva I. Landis, and he had an eighteen-year-old sister named Nadene. His home was a farm in rural Pennsylvania. He said that he'd been in the Army since March 1943, and had come to Europe in November 1944, with the 558th Anti-aircraft Artillery in England, France, Belgium and Holland. He was involved in combat, guarding airports and bridges. He had received the American, European, African and Middle Eastern

Campaign medals, the Good Conduct medal, and the World War II Victory medal. When the war ended, he was sent to Berlin with the occupation troops, and stationed at the Templehof Airbase.

Ardell and I dated every day for five months. We were drawn together from the very beginning, as if we'd known each other our entire lives. Even though there was a language barrier, we soon became best friends. He was so sweet and sincere. We often went to the movies, or sat in a quaint café located down the street and owned by an elderly couple.

Restaurants and bars had to close at 9:00 p.m., but the curfew for civilians wasn't until 11:00 p.m. The owners of the café we frequented closed it at 9:00 p.m., but allowed regular customers and friends to stay and play cards. Since they liked Ardell and me, they said we were welcome to stay if we wished, and sit alone in a booth.

On Saturdays, there was dancing and entertainment in the GI Club at the Templehof Airbase, where Ardell was stationed. We spent a lot of time with his GI friends, Tony and Jim, and their German dates. Ardell didn't care to dance, but we still had a lot of fun.

At 11:00 p.m., Ardell always walked me home. He could have ridden on an army truck back to the airbase at 10:30 p.m., but

ARDELL LANDIS

preferred to spend the extra half hour with me, and walk back to base himself. It was a thirty to forty-five minute trek through deserted, bombed-out streets, and a large park covered with fallen trees. There were disabled tanks and cannons along the way. We heard tales of robberies, assaults, and killings taking place in deserted areas such as these. Ardell took quite a chance walking alone, but he insisted. I always prayed that no harm would come to him. He would laugh about it and assure me that nothing bad would happen.

Before I met Ardell, I had purchased some white linen bed sheets from a distant relative who hadn't lost all her belongings during the war. With her help, I made a white pleated skirt, and a white bush jacket with short sleeves. That was the outfit I was wearing when I met Ardell. It was his favorite outfit, and he loved to see me in it. I was so proud of it, because most of us had nothing nice to wear after the war. However, this outfit was very difficult to keep clean. The soap we used in those days was like clay. I had to scrub my outfit on a washboard and often scraped my knuckles.

In February 1946, Ardell told me that he received orders to return to the United States for discharge. We were both extremely sad and upset. He said he would sign up to stay longer, but that his Dad needed him to work in the gas station while he farmed. When we realized that we might never see each other again, we knew we had fallen in love. We didn't want to lose each other, so Ardell asked me if I would be willing to come to America to marry him. I told him that I would marry him if it was at all possible. It was a lot to think about.

The last Saturday at the Club, while our friends Tony and Jim were dancing with their dates, Ardell slipped me a note. He told me again in this note that he loved me very much and wanted me to come to the United States to marry him. I wrote back that I loved him very much too, and yes, I would marry him. When our friends returned from the dance floor, we told them of our plans. They were very happy and hopeful for us. Ardell kept the proposal note. I found it years later in the safe and cherish it to this day.

After Ardell left Berlin, it was a very sad time for me. I missed him so much. It was almost as if he had died, because I didn't know if we would ever see each other again. Our future was very uncertain, and as far as we knew at the time, it could have taken up to ten years for a German citizen to be allowed to travel to the United States to marry an American.

LAST NIGHT AT THE CLUB
This photo was taken on the last night together at the GI Club, where Ardell proposed to Edith. They are sitting together (back left) and celebrating with Tony, Jim and their German dates.

There was no American Consulate set up in Berlin, and German mail could not be sent directly to the United States. Ardell arranged for Tony to send my letters to him through Army mail, and Ardell would send his letters to me, via U.S. mail, to Tony in Berlin. In order to understand Ardell's letters, and to write my letters to him,

---

HORACE W. VOUGHT
DISTRICT ATTORNEY
MIDDLEBURG, PENNA.

STATE of PENNSYLVANIA
COUNTY of SNYDER

Personally appeared before me a notary public, Ardell L. Landis, of Mt. Pleasant Mills, Snyder County, Pennsylvania, being duly sworn according to law, doth depose and say; that he has agreed to marry Edith Quabeck, of Berlin Germany, and that the said marriage will be concluded within three months after Edith Quabeck's arrival in the United States; that he is twenty-two (22) years of age, has not previously been married and that he is not under any legal disability which would prevent his marriage to Edith Quabeck.

SWORN to and subscribed before
me this_____day of October, 1946.

My Commission Expires

INTENT TO MARRY

Affidavit from Horace W. Vought, DIstrict Attorney, stating Ardell's intent to marry Edith.

I had to use a German/American dictionary for translation. The mailing arrangement worked for a while, until Tony told me that he was being discharged. He asked one of the new guys who was replacing him if he'd be willing to continuing sending our mail back and forth. He said he would, providing I showed him around Berlin. I told Tony to tell him no, thank you, I'd find another way, but for a long time, Ardell and I had no communication. A few months later, I was working part-time in a store and I noticed that a certain GI quite often visited the store with the same German girl. I figured that since he had a steady girlfriend he wouldn't be interested in me, so one day I asked him if he would send a letter for me to Ardell by U.S. Army mail. He replied that he would send one letter on my behalf, and if Ardell answered, he would then continue to send our mail back and forth.

Ardell wrote back immediately after receiving my letter. He wondered if I had changed my mind for some reason, because he hadn't heard from me in so long. He told me that he had gone to see the district attorney, Horace W. Vought, in April. He asked Mr. Vought to write to the immigration service in Washington, D.C., to find out how soon I could come to the United States to be married. He also

```
- 4 - 325
Rev. 8-23-46
```
U. S. DEPARTMENT OF JUSTICE
Immigration and Naturalization Service
Post Office Building
Wilkes Barre, Pa.

Public Law 471, approved June 29, 1946, provides that an alien fiancee or fiance of a United States citizen who is serving in, or who has been honorably discharged from the armed forces of the United States during World War II, may on or before July 1, 1947 be admitted to the United States upon presentation of a Section 3(2) passport visa, as a non-immigrant temporary visitor, for a period of three months, provided:

a. The alien is not subject to exclusion under the immigration laws.
b. The non-preference portion of the quota to which the alien is chargeable is exhausted at the time the alien applies for a visa.
c. The alien is found to be coming to the United States with a bona fide intention of being married to a United States citizen who is serving in, or who has been honorably discharged from the armed forces of the United States during World War II.
d. The administrative authorities are satisfied that a valid marriage can and will be concluded during the period for which the alien is admitted.

Evidence to be furnished the American Consul by such an alien in support of a Section 3(2) visa application shall include sworn statements of both parties indicating they have entered into a valid agreement to marry and that they are legally able and actually willing to conclude a valid marriage within three months after the alien's arrival.

As a requisite to the admission of an alien under this Act, the prospective citizen spouse of such alien shall furnish a bond in the sum of $500, which, in effect, will guarantee that a valid marriage will be concluded within three months or that the alien will leave the United States within that time without expense to the Government. The bond may be furnished by a surety company or secured by a Treasury Bond and posted at the port of arrival or the nearest office of the Immigration and Naturalization Service, but only after the alien has arrived in the United States.

In some instances an alien fiancee or fiance may arrive in the United States in possession of a regualr quota immigration visa for permanent residence. In such cases the above-mentioned bond will not be required. Therefore, the question as to whether a bond must be posted can not be determined until the alien arrives in the United States.

Before issuing a passport visa, the American Consul may wish to satisfy himself that the alien, while awaiting marriage in the United States, will not become a public charge. Therefore, the person who intends to sponsor the alien might forward to the alien for submission to the nearest American Consul an affidavit, in duplicate, showing his income, property, savings, number of dependents, plans and arrangements made for alien's support, etc. If such affidavit is forwarded, it would be well to have it accompanied by affidavits, in duplicate, from the sponsor's employer and the financial institution in which his savings are held tending to support the statements made in his own affidavit.

It is understood that, in general, the alien fiancee or fiance will be required to submit the following to the American Consul:

1. A valid passport good for travel to the United States.
2. Three passport photographs, 2½ inches square, on thin unglazed paper with a light background, full face without head covering. No others may be accepted.

PUBLIC LAW 471

Public Law 471, also known as the "German War Bride Law," was approved on June 29, 1946, and stated that alien fiancees may be granted admission to the United States on or before July 1, 1947.

American Consul
Berlin, Germany.

Dear sir:

I was discharged from the United States Army on the 17th day of March, 1946, after having served three years therein, about half of which time was spent outside the continental limits of the United States.

While serving with the occupation forces in Berlin Germany I met and fell in love with Edith Quabeck, of Berlin. We are engaged to be married and will be married shortly after she arrives in this country in the event permission for her entry is granted.

Enclosed herewith is an affidavit from my bank setting forth my financial position. An affidavit is also enclosed from my father setting forth his financial position.

At the present time I am employed by my father, Lester L. Landis, on his farm and in his gasoline service station at Mt. Pleasant Mills, Snyder County, Pa. My parents have converted their large farm house into a double house in comtemplation of my marriage so that we will have a home in which to live immediately after we are married. My father pays me $20.00 per week at the present time in addition to board and lodging. I also have access to the produce and meat produced on the farm. In other words, the $20.00 per week which I receive is net after living expenses have been provided for.

I was not injured or disabled in the war service and therefore do not receive any disability compensation from the United States Government.

As stated above I intend to marry Miss Quabeck within a short time after she arrives in this country and will be responsible for her care and support.

Very truly yours,

LETTER OF INTENT

Ardell's letter stating his intentions to marry Edith Quabeck.

PALMER E. DINIUS
SHERIFF
OF SNYDER COUNTY
MIDDLEBURG, PA.

TO WHOM IT MAY CONCERN:

    I, Palmer E. Dinius, duly elected Sheriff of Snyder County, Pennsylvania, do hereby certify that I have examined the police records and the Court records of Snyder County, Pennsylvania, with respect to Ardell L. Landis, of Mt. Pleasant Mills, Snyder County, Pennsylvania, and find that the said Ardell L. Landis has not been arrested or charged with any commission of any crime in Snyder County, Pennsylvania. I do further certify that the said Ardell L. Landis bears an excellent reputation in his community for good moral character, industry and integrity.

                                      Palmer E. Dinius, Sheriff of
                                      Snyder County, Pennsylvania.

AFFIDAVIT OF CRIMINAL RECORD

Affidavit from the Sheriff, Palmer E. Dinius, stating that Ardell had no existing criminal record.

inquired about what papers needed to be filed, and what procedures we needed to follow. The answer he received was that, in the near future, a new law would be passed allowing German women to come to America to marry former soldiers. Public Law 471 was passed. It was referred to as the *German War Bride Law*. Ardell needed to begin the paperwork immediately in order to speed up the process.

    Ardell corresponded, via Mr. Vought, with the U.S. Department of Justice, Immigration and Naturalization Service. He received a letter informing him of all the steps he needed to take in

THE ÆTNA CASUALTY AND SURETY COMPANY
HARTFORD, CONNECTICUT
AFFILIATE OF
ÆTNA LIFE INSURANCE COMPANY
THE AUTOMOBILE INSURANCE COMPANY
THE STANDARD FIRE INSURANCE COMPANY

HARRISBURG OFFICE
C. R. WILLIS, MANAGER
TWELFTH FLOOR, STATE STREET BUILDING

HARRISBURG, PA.

November 29, 1946

H. L. Purdy & Son, Agents
Y. M. C. A. Building
Sunbury, Pennsylvania

RE: Ardell Landis
Temporary Alien Bond

Dear Truman:

The Temporary Alien Bond for Ardell Landis is now filed with the Immigration and Naturalization Service, Philadelphia, Pennsylvania. Mr. Horowitz of the Immigration and Naturalization Service, Pennsylvania Building, 42 S. 15th Street, Philadelphia, Pennsylvania, requested that as soon as Mr. Landis knows the name of the ship on which Miss Suaback is sailing, the Port of embarkation and the port of arrival he is to notify the Immigration and Naturalization Service in Philadelphia and they will immediately send the necessary clearance papers to the port.

Will you please convey this information to Mr. Landis for his guidance?

Yours very truly,

Norman Grimshaw, Supt.,
Bond Department

NG:os

TEMPORARY ALIEN BOND FOR ARDELL LANDIS

Aetna Casualty and Surety Company bond stating that Edith would be cleared by the Immigration and Naturalization Service upon arrival in the U.S.

order to bring me from Germany to the United States. He had to send many documents to the American Consulate in Berlin, as soon as it was established. He needed to provide several affidavits: 1) the county sheriff's statement that he had no criminal record; 2) a statement that he would marry me within three months of my arrival in the United States; 3) a statement that he could support me — his father's statement that he was working for him and the wages paid — and that we would have a place of our own in which to live; and 4) a statement from the president of his bank regarding his bank account, and the president's statement as a character witness. Ardell also had to get a $500 bond in case we didn't get married within three months, at which time I would have to go back to Germany. The bond money would pay for my return trip.

The final step was to secure my transportation to the United States. In order to take advantage of the German War Bride Law, I had to be in the United States on or before July 1, 1947. After that date, the law would no longer be in effect. Because there was no way, at the time, for German fiancees to travel to the United States by boat, Ardell had to purchase an airplane ticket and mail it to me in Berlin. The cost of the ticket was $523.25.

AMERICAN AIRLINES SYSTEM

UNION COMMERCE BUILDING • CLEVELAND 14, OHIO • CHERRY 1901

For Reservations, phone ORCHARD 3300

October 12, 1946

Mr. Ardell L. Landis
Mt. Pleasant Mills,
Pennsylvania

Dear Mr. Landis:

Our New York office has forwarded us your letter in which you enclosed a check for $523.25 for a one way ticket from Berlin to New York for Miss Edith Quabeck.

We have authorized American Overseas Airlines in Berlin to issue this ticket to Miss Quabeck when she calls for it. We are enclosing your receipt for payment of this ticket.

The purchase of this ticket does not guarantee a reservation for Miss Quabeck. Also American Overseas Airlines will not be able to advise the American Consul about the purchase of this ticket but when Miss Quabeck picks up her ticket, she can then take it to the Consul.

American Airlines hopes to be of service to you again in the near future.

Very truly yours,

AMERICAN AIRLINES SYSTEM

jl
Encl.

PLANE TICKET RECEIPT

American Airlines letter and receipt of $523.25 for Edith's plane ticket to New York.

> **SUNBURY, PA., Nov. 14, 1946**
>
> **IN ACCOUNT WITH**
> **H. L. PURDY & SON**
> TRUMAN H. PURDY
> **INSURANCE AND REAL ESTATE**
> ROOM NO. 210. Y. M. C. A. BLDG.
>
> Received of Ardell L. Landis Treasurers Check #12792 of the Snyder County Trust Company for $500.00, being security for Surety Bond of Ardell L. Landis for immigration of Edith Quabeck from Germany –
>
> Received Payment
> 11/14/46
> H. L. Purdy & Son

RECEIPT OF BOND MONEY
$500 bond receipt to secure Edith's immigration from Germany.

While Ardell was busy making these arrangements over in America, I had plenty to deal with at home. My mom, family and friends tried to convince me not to leave Germany. They all pointed out that people in the United States might treat me badly so soon after the war ended. Besides, they said, I was always liked and respected by German men and had even received two other marriage proposals. Although they were nice men, and would have loved me and treated me well, I just didn't have that special love for them that I felt,

Fraulein Eligible for Visa To Wed Civilian in U.S.

By ARTHUR NOYES, *Staff Writer*

BERLIN, Aug. 5—German frauleins who are fiancees of Americans no longer under military jurisdiction are now eligible for visas to the U. S. under a June 29 Congressional law which has authorized American consuls to issue visas so that the couples may marry in America.

American consular officials in Berlin have expressed themselves as confused as to how the fiancees will be able to find transportation to the U. S., because the Army will not make transportation available to German nationals.

It was suggested, however, that if a fraulein is able to purchase a ticket on an American commercial air line and gain permission for travel from the Combined Travel Security Board, a tri-party organization with all but Russian representation, the consul will be able to issue a visa upon the display of the air line ticket on the CTSB.

There is also the problem, it was pointed out, of the frauleins gaining permission to land in the European countries along the air line route to the U. S. At present, one official stated, no German nationals are permitted visas to Belgium or France, both nations being stops for the States-bound air liners.

It was emphasized that the regulations for visas for frauleins do not apply to fiancees of American military personnel or persons under American military law as the European Theater Army Command has forbidden marriages with Germans.

A soldier, however, can become engaged to a German woman here, it was explained, and then return to the U. S. and either be discharged from the Army or sever his Army contract and then be eligible to apply to the State Department for the transport of his fiancee to the U. S.

The Congressional law, which applies to all aliens not included under the American Exclusion Laws, stated that the American must offer a sworn statement of his intentions of marriage, corroborated by other suitable evidence.

It was pointed out that the U. S. military authorities are not in a position to furnish any assistance to fiancees wishing to leave Germany, and that the State Department has instructed the consuls to warn interested persons that the Attorney General is required by the Congressional act to demand and accept the bond posted by the intended American spouse after the arrival of the alien fiancees at port of entry.

The bond would cover the cost of transportation back to Germany if the marriage should not be concluded in the three-months period of the visa.

NEWSPAPER ARTICLE

This article appeared in the newspaper on August 5, 1946, reporting Edith's eligibility to come to the United States to marry Ardell.

UNITED STATES POLITICAL ADVISER
FOR GERMANY

Berlin, September 20, 1946.

Mr. Ardell L. Landis,
Mt. Pleasant Mills, Pennsylvania.

Dear Mr. Landis:

Receipt is acknowledged of your letter dated July, 1946, concerning the immigration to the United States of your fiancee, Miss Edith Quabeck.

Your letter has not been answered until now pending final clarification of the fiancee program.

An information sheet concerning visa applications by fiancees of ex-service men is enclosed. This will outline in part the documents required.

The documents mentioned but not described under sub paragraph 1 include the following: birth certificate, police dossier (Polizeiliches Führungszeugnis), affidavits of support (which you have already sent), and four front view photographs, taken with a light background and approximately 2 in. by 2 in. in size. All documents should be submitted in duplicate.

At present the only way to show availability of transportation to the United States is to purchase a Berlin-New York plane ticket from American Overseas Airlines, La Guardia Field, New York, and to mail that to your fiancee. The cost of this ticket is approximately $450.00. At the present time there is no way for fiancees to travel to the United States by boat.

The statements in sub paragraph 3 must be sworn to before a Notary Public or a German public official. In the event that either you or your fiancee have been previously married, divorce or death certificates must be submitted. In the event that either party is under 21, the permission of both parents, if living, must be submitted in writing and also sworn to before a Notary Public or German official.

Two photostatic

LETTER FROM THE U.S. VISA OFFICE IN GERMANY

This letter to Ardell stated that his 'letter of intent' to marry Edith was received, requested that he purchase a Berlin-New York plane ticket for Edith, and informed him of the various documents required.

-2-

Two photostatic copies of your honorable discharge certificate should be submitted.

There is a charge of $10.00, payable only in American currency or money order, for each visa issued. I would suggest that you mail this money order directly to this office. It should be made payable to the Treasurer of the United States.

You are warned that from four to six weeks are usually required for German Nationals to obtain the Exit Permit mentioned in the information sheet.

A copy of this letter is being sent to your fiancee for her information.

Yours very truly,

A. E. Hanney,
Vice Consul,
Chief of Visa Office.

Enclosure:
Information Sheet

File No. 811.11

JTR:shk

LETTER FROM THE VISA OFFICE — PAGE TWO

and still feel, for Ardell. However, in spite of my strong feelings for Ardell, it was very difficult to leave my family and friends in Germany to travel to America and an uncertain future. The only thing I was certain of was that Ardell loved me, and I loved him.

CHAPTER 12

Leaving Berlin

I never received any formal English lessons. In those days, the English language was not taught in schools, so I took lessons from an English tutor twice a week for a month before leaving Germany. I quit when I discovered that the tutor was from England and therefore pronounced many English words differently than Americans. I decided to wait until I got to the United States to learn the language, so I could hear the correct pronunciation. I knew that people would laugh at the way I spoke, but they would eventually get used to it.

In July 1946, while waiting to hear from the American Consulate in Berlin, I went looking for a job because my previous job had ended. I went to the German unemployment office where a very stern, elderly lady was sitting behind a desk. I heard her ask those ahead of me if they could speak English, because there were a few jobs available for those who could. I also heard that, in addition to the wages, employees received one good meal each day, which was very important. When my turn came, I told a little white lie and said that I could speak English. To be quite honest, my English was very limited. I could only write letters to Ardell, and read his letters to me, with the help of a German-American dictionary.

Five of us were chosen, and sent by subway for an interview. I soon realized that the others could speak perfect English, for some of them had lived in England or America before the war, and others had taught English in school. I didn't reveal to them that I spoke only limited English. When we arrived, and I was called in for my interview, I told the American officer the truth. He simply smiled and said that the job involved sensoring telegrams, and that he actually needed someone to check the *German*-written telegrams. Had I been truthful to the woman at the employment office, she would never even have given me the chance for an interview. I was hired, and worked with American soldiers until I came to the United States. This job proved a great help for me to learn more of the English language.

In October 1946, I received the anxiously-awaited phone call from the American Consulate in Berlin, and I was scheduled for an appointment. I was supposed to bring a letter from the German Police Department stating that I had no police record. I had to have an affidavit from a special office stating that I did not belong to the Nazi Party, or have any charges against me that would prevent my permission to come to the United States. I was required to have a physical examination, and was also cross-examined for approximately four hours by several American officers at the Consulate. One officer looked at my German police report, which had been sealed in an envelope. He opened the envelope and, after reading the document, said, "Miss Quabeck, I see here that you were in jail for five years. Why?" I looked at him with amazement, and assured him that I was never arrested or jailed at any time. He said, "You don't want to make a liar out of me, do you?" I told him of course not, but he must have someone else's report. He wrote something on the document, laid it aside and told me to wait outside.

A short while later, another officer called me in. He said, "Miss Quabeck, you want to go to America to marry an ex GI. Why?" I noticed a wedding ring on his hand, so I told him it was for the

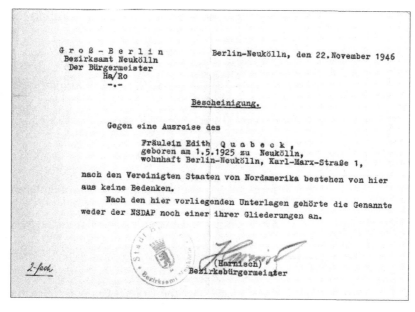

AFFIDAVIT

Document stating that Edith Quabeck had no affiliations with the Nazi Party, or any charges against her that would prevent acceptance into the United States.

same reason he probably got married — because Ardell and I loved each other. Then he said, "Yes, but you say you want to marry this man, and yet two of my soldiers saw you on October 3rd, walking down the street close to your house between two American GIs."

By then, I was very puzzled and annoyed by what was occurring. I told him that I had never dated an American soldier, before or after Ardell. He said, "You don't want to make a liar out of me, do you?" I told him no, but that they must have seen a different girl. The officer proceeded to write something on the document, and told me to wait outside.

In the waiting room I spoke to several other German girls, and some of them were very upset. They felt they had been rudely treated. I decided to keep my cool. I had nothing to worry about. If they had the wrong information it would just have to be straightened out. I could not say that the officers were rude. They were just very sober and official in their manner.

After another hour of waiting, the Consul General called me in to his office. He told me that he had reviewed all the documents I submitted, and everything was in order. He apologized for the cross-examination by the other officers, and explained to me that it was necessary to ask why I had been jailed for five years, because if I *had* been in jail for anything at all, I no doubt would have argued that it was a *lesser* amount of time. That way, they could trick me into admitting that I indeed *was* in jail. When the officer made up the story that I was seen walking down the street between two Americans, he did so to make certain that I wanted to go to the United States for the right reason. His exact words were, "We want to be sure, because we don't want any 'undesirables' to get into the United States."

The Consul General assured me that everything was fine and they would be honored to have me come to the United States. We shook hands, and he said he hoped I would be very happy and like it there. As I was leaving, I saw the other officers in the hall. They smiled at me and wished me good luck.

The Consul General informed me that I might be able to leave Germany sometime in December, but it could be later. I told Ardell in a letter that it could be as late as March of 1947 until I would see him. In the beginning of December 1946, since we had no idea when I would be leaving, several of my friends and relatives held a farewell party for me. Many of them wrote poems for me, and the children drew pictures. It was very emotional for all of us. I will always treasure everything I received that day, and have it preserved in my scrapbook.

CERTIFICATE OF IDENTITY IN LIEU OF PASSPORT 20448

U. S. Consulate General, Berlin, Germany

Date December 11, 1946

1. This is to certify that **Edith Vera Quabeck** (name in full), born at Germany (country), Berlin (town), Neukoelln (district), on 1st (day) of May (month), 1925 (year), Female (sex), Single (marital status) _____ (given & maiden name of wife), intends to immigrate to United States of America

2. He (she) will be accompanied by _____
(Here list all family members by name, birthplace & date, together with citizenship of each)

3. His (her) occupation is Office Clerk

4. DESCRIPTION

Height 5 ft. 5 in.

Hair Brown Eyes Grey-Blue

Distinguishing marks or features:
None

record for the following reason(s) _____

I hereby certify that the above are true facts, proper photograph and description of

Edith Vera Quabeck
(Signature of applicant)

Service No:
No Fee Prescribed V-3379

(Signature of consul)
Subscribed and sworn to
December 11, 1946
(Date)

CERTIFICATE OF IDENTITY IN LIEU OF PASSPORT

This document certified Edith Quabeck's intent to immigrate to the United States.

CHAPTER 13

Arrival in America

On December 13, 1946, I got an unexpected phone call from the American Consulate. They told me that seven GIs had to stay in Berlin, and seven German war brides could take their places on the plane. Since my documents were in order, and my plane ticket had been paid for, I could leave that very evening. I decided to take advantage of the opportunity. The waiting had been hard on all of us, and this way, I wouldn't have long to think about it. Furthermore, I didn't know when there would be another seat available on a plane because so many GIs were going home.

I had to obtain a Certificate of Identification in Lieu of Passports, Military Exit Permit, and a Security Clearance. My family

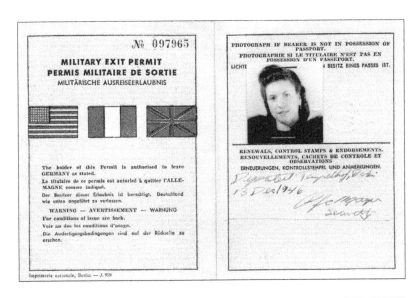

MILITARY EXIT PERMIT

Document permitting the bearer, Edith Quabeck, to leave Berlin, Germany. It was dated December 9, 1946, and used for her departure on December 13, 1946.

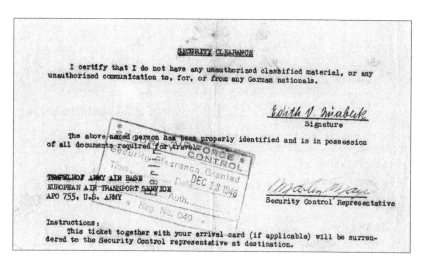

SECURITY CLEARANCE

Certificate stating that Edith did not have in her possession any unauthorized classified material, or communications from German Nationals.

accompanied me to the airport. It was very hard on all of us. I'll never forget my nephew Wolfgang, for he was like a little brother to me. He was five years old, and screamed as I walked to the plane, "Please don't leave, Tante Edith, please don't leave!" It was heart breaking. My sister later wrote that he didn't want to eat anything, and couldn't sleep for over a week.

When I left Berlin, I was told that a telegram would be sent to Ardell from the airport in Berlin, stating the time of my arrival in New York. We flew from Berlin to Iceland, then to Canada, and landed at LaGuardia Field, New York, on Saturday, December 14, 1946. We

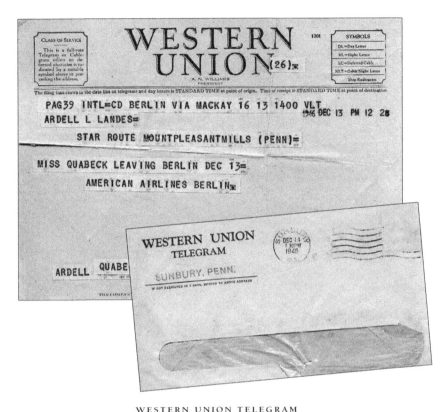

WESTERN UNION TELEGRAM
The telegram confirming Edith's departure from Berlin on December 13, 1946.

were the only seven girls on the plane, and I was the only one going to Pennsylvania. The flight from Berlin to New York took twenty-three hours because we traveled in a four-engine plane, not a jet airliner. There were two layovers — one in Iceland and another in Canada.

We were the first seven German war brides to come to the United States after World War II, and when we landed in New York

AMERICAN AIRLINES TICKET AND BAGGAGE TRANSFER

PHILADELPHIA RECORD

The first seven war brides arrived on Saturday, December 14, 1946.
This photo and article appeared the following Monday. Edith is at the top of the steps.

CHICAGO SUNDAY TRIBUNE

This photograph appeared on January 5, 1947. Edith is sitting fourth from the left.

City, newspaper reporters and photographers were waiting to interview us and take our pictures. Our photographs were published in many major newspapers throughout the United States.

When we got off the plane, the fiancés of the other six girls were there waiting for them, but Ardell wasn't there waiting for me. He had never received the telegram informing him that I was coming. Again and again his name was announced over the loudspeaker. Finally, they called me into an office to talk to a German-speaking officer from the Immigration Department. They were very nice and willing to assist me. They tried to obtain Ardell's address and phone number, but could not locate the town of Mt. Pleasant Mills, PA on the map. I remembered Ardell mentioning the city of Harrisburg at one point, but had no idea how far it was from his home. His phone number, at that time, was listed as a Selinsgrove number, though his address was Mt. Pleasant Mills. When I told them this, I pronounced Selinsgrove incorrectly, so they still couldn't figure out how to reach Ardell. I couldn't pronounce Ardell correctly, either, because I always called him by his nickname, "Tom." When I said his real name, they thought I said "Allen" instead of Ardell. We had quite a time until it was all straightened out.

A man from immigration asked if I had any American money in my possession. I told him that I had ten dollars, which Ardell had sent in case of an emergency. In those days, ten dollars was quite a lot of money. Ardell wanted to be sure that I had enough money for a snack at the airport, in case his plane arrived in New York later than mine. He never imagined that he would not even be in New York to greet me! The man from immigration said that he was sorry, but he had to take eight dollars as "Alien Head Tax" to get into the country. I was left with only two dollars.

The first officer I spoke to explained how there was no plane leaving that evening from Harrisburg, Pennsylvania for New York

CUSTOMS RECEIPT
American Airlines receipt of payment of Alien Head Tax

City, so Ardell would not be able to come for me. The officer stated that he could arrange for my stay in a New York hotel, using the Traveler's Aid fund, but decided against it since I spoke little English. There was a plane leaving that night at 9:00 p.m. from Newark, New Jersey to Harrisburg. He said he would personally loan me money for the ticket if I thought Ardell would send him a money order on Monday to repay him. I assured him that he would be reimbursed.

He called Ardell to explain everything, but before he could talk to him, there was yet another mix up. Ardell was working at the gas station when the call came, and his brother-in-law, Palmer, answered the phone at home. Palmer thought the caller wanted *Allen*

Landis, so he told him he had a wrong number and hung up. The officer called back, and made it clear that he wanted to speak to *Ardell* Landis. Palmer quickly got Ardell from the gas station and the officer explained everything. He promised Ardell that he would personally see to it that I got to the Harrisburg Airport, and told him what time he could pick me up.

The officer came to my assistance one last time. I needed to travel by taxi from LaGuardia Field, New York to the Newark airport in New Jersey, to board the plane for Harrisburg, Pennsylvania. He took me to the taxi, explained everything to the driver, and told me to pay the driver with the two remaining dollars that I had. Another female passenger rode in the taxi with me. During the trip to Newark, she talked non-stop. Once we arrived, I could see by her expression that she had been asking me questions, but I hadn't understood a word she'd said. When I tried to explain to her that I could not speak English, she looked very disappointed. At the Newark airport, the taxi driver took me to a stewardess, who spoke German, and told me to stay by her side. She would be on the flight to Harrisburg with me.

Finally, at 9:00 p.m. Saturday, I was on the final leg of my journey. When I arrived in Harrisburg, Ardell was waiting there for

TWA AIRLINE TICKET AND BAGGAGE CLAIM
TWA ticket for flight from Newark, New Jersey to Harrisburg, Pennsylvania on December 14, 1946.

me with his sister and brother-in-law, Nadene and Palmer Pyle. It was a very happy reunion, just like a dream. He kept telling me over and over how sorry he was that he didn't meet me at the airport in New York. I told him that it wasn't his fault, it couldn't be helped, and everything worked out just fine. After all the time apart, and the many complications we'd encountered, we were finally reunited. It had been ten long months since Ardell and I had last seen each other.

On the way home from the airport, we stopped at a restaurant and I was treated to my first banana split, which, at that time, cost only twenty-five cents.

The telegram sent from Berlin, stating the date and time of my arrival in New York, came two days after I was with Ardell in Pennsylvania. My suitcase had been sent to Pittsburgh by mistake, and was then forwarded by train to Middleburg, a small town a few miles from Mt. Pleasant Mills. I received it four days later. During that weekend, Ardell's sister loaned me some of her clothing, and the following Monday Ardell bought me some new things. I guess it is true what they say — "Love conquers all!"

Shortly after the photographs of our arrival at LaGuardia Field were published in the newspapers, we heard from Ardell's army buddy, Jim, who lived in Philadelphia. He recognized my picture in the newspaper and sent a telegram welcoming me to America, and congratulating both of us. We stayed in touch with Jim and another army buddy, Tony, who lived in Pittsburgh. They both came to visit us several times, and we continued to write to each other. Jim and Tony each married American girls after returning from the war.

Ardell received letters from nine ex-GIs in different states asking him how he'd managed to get his fiancee over here so quickly. They wondered if he could give them advice on how to do the same. Ardell wrote to every one of them.

The Landis family owned a big farmhouse and fixed it up into a two-family home. We had one half of the house to ourselves, which was very nice.

Exactly two weeks after my arrival, Ardell and I were married at 8:00 p.m. on Saturday, December 28, 1946, in the living room of his parent's home. Nadene and Palmer stood up for us, and Ardell's parents and a few relatives were present. I was very nervous because they were all strangers to me. I had mixed feelings. On one hand, I was filled with joy to be marrying Ardell; and on the other, I was very sad that my family couldn't be there to share in my happiness.

ARDELL AND EDITH LANDIS — WEDDING PICTURE

The Lutheran minister, Reverend Dean, officiated. Since I barely spoke English, the minister instructed that, if he paused to look at me, I should say, "I do." I often tease about that, because I could have sold myself to China and wouldn't have known it.

Ardell's family made me feel very welcomed from the start. His father spoke Pennsylvania-Dutch, which many people thought was similar to the German language. However, I speak High German, which is somewhat different. The Pennsylvania-Dutch language was a slight help, but many of the words are different. I made friends very quickly, and everyone I met treated me wonderfully. Ardell's father

NADENE (ARDELL'S SISTER) AND PALMER PYLE

ARDELL'S PARENTS, MELVA AND LESTER LANDIS

THE LANDIS FARM HOUSE

Following their marriage, Ardell and Edith resided in this farm house located in Mt. Pleasant Mills, Pennsylvania.

owned the gas station, and a lot of men would spend time loafing there. Ardell worked long hours while his dad was running the farm. I went to the gas station quite often to spend time with Ardell. I soon found out that many of the people from this area were descended from German backgrounds.

In Berlin, we always dressed up on Sundays, wearing high heels and nylons, so that is how I dressed on Sundays when I went to the gas station. Ardell was very proud of the way I looked. I was very happy; but for a long time after I arrived in America, I continued to relive the war. At night, when I heard the sirens of a fire truck or an ambulance, I would jump out of bed, thinking it was an air raid.

THE GAS STATION
Edith sometimes tended the pumps at the gas station, which was owned by Ardell's father.

CHAPTER 14

The Big Adjustment

Shortly after my arrival in Pennsylvania, Ardell introduced me to his friends, Paul and Ruth Arbogast, who had married a short time before we did. We quickly became good friends and had lots of fun together, especially on weekends, when Ardell had more free time. Over the years we became almost like family, and we still get together today.

I remember in the beginning, when I got lonely or homesick, friends would visit me. After our oldest daughter Janet was born, I would pull her in a little wagon over the hill to visit my friend Arlene and her family. Sometimes Arlene and another friend, Lorena, came to visit me. I don't think either of them realized how much their friendship meant to me, and still does.

Marlin and Arlene Sierer and their three children.

Ruth and Paul Arbogast and their daughter, Darlene.

I was very happy here from the start. Everyone was so nice to me. We have a saying in Germany: "the way you call into the woods the echo comes back." I believe that. Usually, the way you act towards others causes them to respond in a similar way. In spite of warnings from my family and friends in Germany — that I might be treated badly so soon after the war — I was not worried. I thought that, if people were so narrow-minded and held the war against me, I could do without their friendship. We Germans had suffered a lot from American air raids. War was hell for everyone involved, and I just thanked God it was over.

Gradually my English improved and, though I made an awful lot of mistakes, I managed to communicate quite well. Initially, I would try to explain what I meant by describing the shape of the object and the material it was made of. On one such occasion, at a drive-in restaurant, I wanted to buy an ice cream cone. Since I didn't know the word for "cone," I just asked the waitress for ice cream. She asked me if I wanted a cup or a sundae. I kept saying "no," but she insisted that was all she had. I then told her that I wanted a "waffle tube." She said she didn't have anything like that either. I explained that I saw a lady eating one in her car. She looked over and realized what I was trying to say. I finally got my ice cream cone, and I'm sure she had a good laugh when I left.

One day Ardell and I drove his dad's old 1934 Chevy. We were taking his cousin Anna Lee home to Milton, a town thirty miles away. The car had a habit of jerking, and as we drove north on Routes 11 & 15, the car jerked several times. Anna Lee said, "Let me get out and push." Now, in German, "pusch" is a slang term for "urinate." I didn't connect her remark with the car, and thought she had to go to the bathroom. I kept saying to Ardell, "not here along the road!" Finally, Ardell asked me what I was talking about. When I told him what I thought Anna Lee meant, we all had a good laugh!

After I had been here for eleven months, our first daughter, Janet, was born November 22, 1947, in the Lewistown Hospital. I felt pretty lonely at times, because Ardell worked such long hours, and she was a Godsend. She was really the only thing in my life that I could call my own. My whole world revolved around her.

At that time, mothers who had given birth were supposed to stay in the hospital for ten days. Those who lived in town, however, were able to go home a few days earlier by ambulance if they wished. I asked the doctor if I could possibly leave the hospital, and go home by car, on the sixth day. He said it would be all right if I promised to take it easy for a while.

So many English words still sounded alike to me, and I often mixed things up. The day of my discharge, a nurse came in to my room with a list of names, and told me I had to have an "enema." I thought she meant an "ambulance," it sounded so similar to me. I told her that the doctor said I didn't have to take it. She said my name was on her list. I told her that I would just stay a few more days then. She assured me that it wouldn't make any difference, and she could not understand why I was suddenly acting so stubborn on the last day. I finally told her that I didn't want it because it was "just for show." She realized then that we were talking about two completely different things, and she asked me what I was referring to. I told her, "Oh, such a sick wagon!" She started laughing, and told me that she was talking about making my bowels move. She said, "Honey, I promise you, I'll put a screen around your bed, so it will not be a show!" Of course, I had been picturing the idea of arriving back in Mt. Pleasant Mills by ambulance as "a show." In no time, it was a big joke among the doctors and nurses at the hospital that "Mrs. Landis didn't want an 'enema' for a show."

As far as reading, writing, and spelling were concerned, I taught myself by looking through catalogs, books, and the funnies pages in the newspaper. Though my English wasn't very good, I immediately liked life in America. I had been born and raised in a city, but I just loved living in the country.

Ardell and I had always planned on having two or three children, but I was hoping to be able to visit Berlin at least one more time before that. When my English improved, and Janet started going to school, I decided to get a job to earn money for the trip. I worked in a shirt factory and a dress factory.

We sent many care packages to my mother in Germany, including more than thirty boxes of clothing donated by members of our church, St. John's Lutheran Church, in Mt. Pleasant Mills. After the war, German people couldn't get very much of anything, and this clothing was distributed to many thankful people upon its arrival.

In January 1950, I became a citizen of the United States. In November of the same year, my mother came from Berlin to live with us. We lived on a farm, and our side of the house faced the barn. One day my mom looked out the window and she said to me, "Edith, how can a young girl like you get used to this? All you see is chickens!" Of course, it was different for me, because I was in love. When I looked out our windows, I saw so much more than just chickens!

We thought that, by bringing my mom to live with us, we could offer her a better life. However, after a few short months, she began to feel homesick and wanted to return to Berlin. She couldn't speak English and she missed the city. She told us that my sister Luzie needed her, because she was to have an operation and mom felt she should be there to take care of Luzie's two boys. She said she enjoyed being with us, and that everyone made her feel very welcomed. She realized that I was happy and shared a good life with Ardell and our daughter Janet, who was then three years old. So she made up her mind to go home to Berlin. Every few weeks she would ask me if I had told Ardell about her plans. Actually, I had not mentioned anything to him, because I was secretly hoping she would change her mind. Besides, it would cost a lot of money to send her back to Germany. Then one day, she said to me, "I want to go home, even if I have to swim back!" That was the day I finally told Ardell her wishes. She had some health problems, so we took her to a doctor. His advice was that it would be best to let her return to Berlin, since she was so homesick. She did return home, but after she had been back in Berlin for a few months, she sent me letters saying that she wished she had stayed with us in America. What could I say? It had been her decision to return home. My mother was sixty-six years old when she was here with us in America. She died in Berlin at the age of eighty-six.

CHAPTER 15

The Final Chapter

By 1955, I had saved enough money working in the shirt and dress factories. With a little financial help from Ardell, I took Janet, then seven years old, along with me on a trip to Berlin to meet the rest of my family. In those days, it was much cheaper to travel by ship. We sailed on the *Italia*, and we shared our cabin with another couple. It took nine days for us to sail across the Atlantic Ocean to Europe, and eleven days to return. The weather was stormy several times throughout the trip, and I would get seasick. After traveling by ship to Hamburg, Germany, we flew to Berlin. We had a very pleasant stay. Janet played with the children, and picked up a bit of the German language. When we arrived home, however, she refused to continue speaking it. As an adult, she wishes I had been more insistent that she learn the German language, but I never wanted to force it on any of my children.

After the trip to Berlin, Ardell and I decided to have one or two more children, if possible. We hoped for at least one son in the bunch, and on June 10, 1957, we were blessed with our son, Steve. Janet was then nine and a half years old. Three years later, on January 29, 1960, our youngest daughter, Debbie, was born, and she was such a joy. Our dreams had come true. We now had the family we always wanted.

The Landis family: (clockwise from top) Ardell, Edith, Steve, Debbie and Janet.

We felt very blessed to have three wonderful children. They all grew up to be fine, compassionate, loving people, and we are very proud of them. They've given us four grandsons. Janet and the late Lynn Hackenberg had two sons, Bruce and Mick. (In 1985, Lynn was killed in an automobile accident.) Debbie and her husband Keith Shaffer have a son, Justin; and Steve has one son, Brock. We are a very close-knit family, and I feel very fortunate that all of our children and grandchildren live nearby. They are a great help to me, and a huge source of comfort. Not a day goes by without one of them stopping in to visit.

In 1961, my nephew Wolfgang came over to visit us for six months. He was nineteen years old. I visited Berlin again, alone, in 1965. By this time the Berlin Wall had been built, dividing the city in half. East Berlin was under Russian occupation, and West Berlin was under American, British and French occupation.

There was, at first, a barbed wire fence, which was patrolled by the Russians day and night. Later, at night, they began to construct a concrete wall over eight feet high through the city. People were no longer able to travel between the East and West sides. During that time, I received information and newspaper clippings from my relatives in Berlin. Entire families had been separated by the wall. If someone happened to be on the East side, visiting a friend, they were not permitted to return home to their family on the West side. They used an entire block of houses as a division line the first few days. The people who lived in these houses had their back doors and windows in the Russian Sector, and their front doors and windows in the American Sector.

THE BERLIN WALL
In the initial stages, apartment houses and buildings became division lines, and were bricked up as part of the Berlin Wall.

On the first day, fire trucks from the American Sector came with ladders and nets to help people jump out of windows and escape to the West side. I received a letter from my mom with a newspaper clipping. The article reported that an eighty-seven-year-old woman had jumped from a second floor window into a net, which the firemen had spread fifteen feet below. In her arms, she clutched her cat. Police from the Russian-controlled East Sector heard people

DARING ESCAPE

An old woman's escape, out the window and into the West side, was caught on camera.

from the West Sector yelling, "Grandma, jump!" over and over. The noise alerted the Communist German police. They kicked in the door of her apartment, and two of them tried to pull her back inside. A young man from the West Sector climbed onto a ground-floor windowsill. Held by policemen, he reached up and grabbed the woman's leg and tried pulling her down, while the communist police officers were pulling her upwards by her one arm. In her other arm, she still held the cat! Finally, she threw the cat into the net and jumped. It was really amazing. Fortunately, she only slightly injured her hip. Four other residents from that street were not so lucky. One missed the net, and the other three jumped without any net. Four wooden crosses now mark the sidewalk where they died.

In a few days, the entire block of that street was evacuated, and the windows were bricked shut. Like everywhere else along the wall, there was a large section of "no man's land." Nobody could get close enough to try climbing over the wall to the West side. There were towers with searchlights and guards on the Communist side, and they would shoot anyone who tried to escape to the West side.

In March 1963, I received a newspaper clipping from Berlin telling about a friend of mine, Horst Klein, who had escaped. He and

FRITZ KLEIN FAMILIE — TRAPEZE ARTISTS

Horst Klein, a member of this family of trapeze artists and long-time friend of Edith, managed a daring escape over the Berlin Wall using power lines.

his family, the "Fritz Klein Familie," were well-known trapeze artists in a large circus. Horst and I were very close friends throughout our childhood and afterwards. He and his family had toured in eighteen different countries, and he was one of the best-known performers in Europe. He was a resident of West Berlin, but while appearing in East Berlin, the Communists put a blockade into effect and began erecting the Berlin Wall.

Since Horst was well known for his anti-Communist beliefs, he was forced to give up his occupation as a performer and work in a factory. For many months, he secretly planned his escape — he would crawl over the wall under the protection of darkness. On December 27, 1962, he walked to the wall, carrying a rope. He then discovered an alarm wire on the wall, and, at the spur of the moment, climbed a large electric light pole, with 110,000-volt power lines. He was able to swing around the poles and drop down onto the power lines, which were approximately fifty feet above the ground. He could feel the electricity flowing by the vibration against his legs. Spotlights illuminated everything below, and he could see the East Berlin guards, but, because he was above the spotlights, concealed in darkness, the guards could not see him.

The temperature was below-freezing and his hands swiftly became numb. As he attempted to swing around another pole, he lost his grip and fell to the ground, fifty feet below. Horst landed on the West Berlin side, but was knocked unconscious for three hours. He had fractured both arms, and had internal and head injuries. When he regained consciousness, he realized that he was within shooting range of the East German guards. Luckily, it was still dark. In spite of his condition, he managed to crawl through a small canal in freezing water. The West Berlin rescue squad arrived at the scene to assist him, and he remained in the hospital for a long time. His ordeal became known as one of the most daring escapes since the Communists had erected the wall.

In 1968, I was hired at the Selinsgrove Center for the Mentally Retarded and Epilepsy, and worked there for eighteen years. In 1970, I took Steve, who was thirteen years old, and Debbie, ten and a half years old, to Berlin to meet their grandma and the rest of my family. We had a wonderful time. The children had the chance to see much of West Berlin, which was really being developed.

We visited the Berlin Wall and looked over into East Berlin from little platforms. We could see the Communist guards on their towers with binoculars and guns. It looked so depressing on the East side. As far as one could see, there was nothing but barricades. There were many crosses marking the spots where people had been killed while trying to escape. It was in such contrast to the West Side. I am so thankful that my family lived in the American Sector. Everything there was gradually improving, and the city was being rebuilt.

Steve and Debbie had a good time with the relatives, and enjoyed sightseeing. During our visit, we celebrated my mom's eighty-sixth birthday. I had originally planned this visit for the following year, but decided to go a year earlier instead. I'm so glad that I did, and the children were able to see their grandma, because a few months later, in November, she passed away.

In 1980, and again in 1987, Ardell and I visited Berlin together. He really enjoyed these trips — specifically the family gatherings, sightseeing, and, of course, the German food. He especially enjoyed the delicious breads and pastries. My entire family loved Ardell, and everybody was happy to see him. We had a wonderful time during both trips.

Whenever any of us visited West Berlin, we always stayed with my relatives. It worked out nicely because they would show us around and I, of course, was always the translator. These days the young German people learn English in school and speak it very well.

In 1989, I visited Berlin again when my sister, Luzie, was admitted to a nursing home. She passed away in early 1990. She had been in America several times to visit us. We have had many nieces, nephews, and friends come over throughout the years. We continue to take turns visiting each other, and always have a great time.

In the summer of 1999, my daughter Debbie, my grandson Justin, and I went to Berlin. Justin was able to meet my entire family and he enjoyed the experience very much. The wall had been taken down by then, and we were able to go sightseeing wherever we wished. As always, we stayed at a relative's home.

My daughter Janet, her companion Bud, and two other friends traveled to Germany in 2000, and they visit quite often.

Leaving Germany in 1946 wasn't as emotionally difficult as I had imagined — thinking it was good-bye forever, and I would never see my mother, sister, or anyone in my family again. Everything was so uncertain then, as far as the future was concerned. I didn't know then if I would ever be able to afford returning for a visit. The one true thing I was certain of was Ardell. We loved each other, and we wanted to spend the rest of our lives together. I had no doubt whatsoever that he was a good, decent, honest person. I felt that I knew him well enough to trust that he was sincere, and meant every word he told me. My faith in him was right, and he never disappointed me. Of course, it takes two to make a good marriage, and I did my share. Whatever came along, we faced it together, and had a good, happy life.

My love story, however, has a very sad chapter. In 1996, Ardell was diagnosed with cancer, and he battled it for two years. Our 50th wedding anniversary was approaching — December 28, 1996. We were afraid he might not be with us much longer, after going through thirty-eight grueling radiation treatments and two surgeries. He later experienced kidney failure, and needed to be connected to a dialysis machine three days a week, four hours each day.

To celebrate our 50th wedding anniversary, our children gave us a very nice party for twenty-two guests at a local restaurant, BJ's – A Place for Ribs. Five of my relatives from Berlin traveled to be with us. Ardell enjoyed it very much. He could still maneuver pretty well at this point. With the exception of his treatments and hospital appointments, I took care of him myself the entire time. I wanted him to be at home with his family, in familiar surroundings, until the end.

50TH WEDDING ANNIVERSARY
Edith and Ardell celebrated their 50th wedding anniversary (December 28, 1996) with family and friends at a local restaurant.

On April 7, 1998, Ardell passed away at home. Losing him has been more difficult than anything I've experienced in my life, including the war. I'll never regret, for one moment, my decision to come to this country to marry him. He was a very kind, good-hearted, loving father and husband. Of course, we each did our part to make it a wonderful marriage — we had excellent communication, and very few disagreements. Ours was, indeed, a great love story.

JANET HACKENBERG AND HER COMPANION, HOWARD "BUD" WOLF

JANET'S SON BRUCE HACKENBERG WITH HIS FIANCÉE, TRISH;
AND SON MICK HACKENBERG WITH HIS WIFE, SHANNON

STEVE LANDIS AND HIS SON, BROCK

KEITH AND DEBBIE SHAFFER AND THEIR SON, JUSTIN

PEACHES
*After Ardell died, Edith got this cat to keep her company.
She named her "Peaches" after his favorite fruit.*

Made in the USA
Coppell, TX
26 September 2021